TOWARDS A RADICAL
METAPHYSICS OF SOCIALISM

Towards a Radical Metaphysics of Socialism
Marx and Laruelle

Katerina Kolozova

punctum books * brooklyn, ny

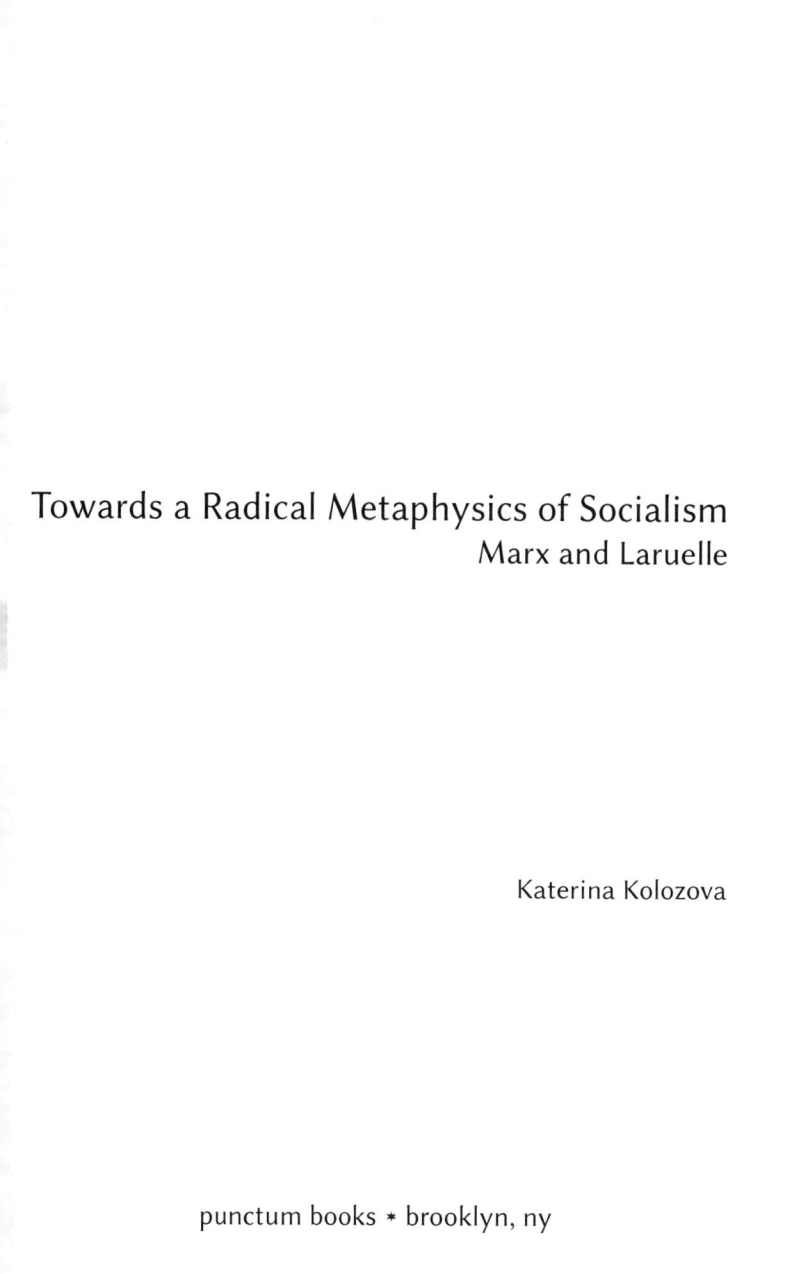

Towards a Radical Metaphysics of Socialism:
Marx and Laruelle
© Katerina Kolozova, 2015.

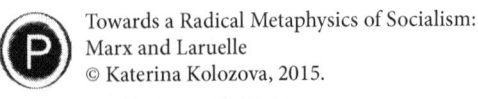

http://creativecommons.org/licenses/by-nc-sa/4.0/

This work carries a Creative Commons BY-NC-SA 4.0 International license, which means that you are free to copy and redistribute the material in any medium or format, and you may also remix, transform and build upon the material, as long as you clearly attribute the work to the authors, you do not use this work for commercial gain in any form whatsoever, and that for any remixing and transformation, you distribute your build under the same license.

First published in 2015 by
punctum books
Brooklyn, New York
http://punctumbooks.com

punctum books is an independent, open-access publisher dedicated to radically creative modes of intellectual inquiry and writing across a whimsical para-humanities assemblage. We solicit and pimp quixotic, sagely mad engagements with textual thought-bodies, and provide shelters for intellectual vagabonds.

The author wishes to thank Eileen A. Joy for supporting this project and Troy O'Neill for editorial help.

Cover Image: UFO House, Sanjhih, Taiwan (2008), Wikimedia Commons

ISBN-13: 978-0692492413
ISBN-10: 0692492410

Facing-page drawing by Heather Masciandaro.

Before you start to read this book,
take this moment to think about making a donation to **punctum books**, an independent non-profit press,

@ http://punctumbooks.com/about/

If you're reading the e-book, you can click on the image below to go directly to our donations site. Any amount, no matter the size, is appreciated and will help us to keep our ship of fools afloat. Contributions from dedicated readers will also help us to keep our commons open and to cultivate new work that can't find a welcoming port elsewhere. Our adventure is not possible without your support.

Vive la open-access.

Fig. 1. Hieronymus Bosch, *Ship of Fools* (1490-1500)

Table of Contents

Image Credits

1: Introduction   1

2: The Possibility of Immanent Revolt as Theory and Political Praxis   21

3: Metaphysics of the Finance Economy   37

4: The Metaphysics of Capitalism and the Socialist Response   57

5: Technology, the Body, and the Materialist Determination in the Last Instance of the Communist Society of "Cyborgs"   91

References   103

Image Credits*

Front Cover: UFO House, Sanjhih, Taiwan (2008), Wikimedia Commons.

Chapter 1: UFO House, Sanjhih, Taiwan (2006) Flikr.

Chapter 2: Roman Bezjak, Bank of Georgia, Tbilisi, Georgia. (2011), Sozialistische Moderne - Archäologie einer Zeit.

Chapter 3: Petrova Gora Monument, Petrova, Croatia (2010), Wikimedia Commons.

Chapter 4: China Central Television Headquarters, Beijing, China (2008), Office of Metropolitan Architecture.

Chapter 5: Ilinden, Kruševo, Republic of Macedonia (2012), Wikimedia Commons.

*Ornamentals at the heading of each chapter are illustrations based on the images listed above.

01: Introduction

I. Estrangement as the Generic Mode of Exploitation

François Laruelle's non-Marxist reading of Marx, executed in *Introduction au non-marxisme*, is accomplished by allowing Marx's text to speak for itself, without placing it into the history of philosophy.[1] A non-philosophical reading of Marx operates with the "use-value" of concepts that have been radicalized to expose their unilateral correlation with the effect of the real. In non-philosophy (also called non-standard philosophy), the "real" is the instance of unilateral, indifferent effect of a radical exteriority with respect to the signifying subject. In other words, one does not refer to the abstraction of "the Real," but rather to concrete instances of an effect of the real, of that which always already escapes signification but is nonetheless out there. In the case of Marx's science of society, the "out there" is the practice of the workforce, the lived of wage labor as envisaged praxis of socialist emancipation. Radical concepts are "affected by the real"; they have "use-value" in the sense that they correlate and effect a reality that is, as Laruelle would say, "lived" and "experienced," or, as Marx would say, a reality that is "physical and sensuous."[2] Philosophical recreation of Marx's thought entails production of "surplus value," assuming an independent "life" and acting as if self-sufficient reality is detached from the material real, which is

---

[1] François Laruelle, *Introduction au non-marxisme* (Paris: Presses Universitaires de France, 2000).
[2] Karl Marx, "Theses on Feuerbach," in Karl Marx and Frederick Engels, *The German Ideology*, trans. Roy Pascal (London: Lawrence and Wishart, 1938), available at http://www.marxists.org/archive/marx/works/1845/theses/.

precisely how capitalism operates.

Following Laruelle, I argue that philosophy is constituted in a fashion perfectly analogous to the one which grounds capitalism—philosophy constitutes a reality in its own right and a reality that establishes an amphibology with the real (acts in its stead, posturing as "more real than the real"). In the split of the physical from the real of sensations of pain and pleasure, the detached body and mind meet in order to produce "material" effects—an instance which we shall call "the real," following the terminology of non-philosophy—which constitutes estrangement as oppression, a characteristic of both philosophy and capitalism. Alienation is at the heart of the great (existentialist) torment of modern Man (therefore, in some form/s, Woman's too), the source of spiritual and physical suffering. Its source, however, is one of the ruses of social reason (i.e., the reason of modernity): the illusion of philosophy and of capitalism about a self-sufficiency and "endowment with reality" that is greater than the reality of the real or of the material, which hasn't been reinvented through reason and technology.

I.1. The Real or the "Interest"

Similarly to Marx's project of creating a science of the political-economic exploitation of human labor, the non-philosophical idea of "the science of the human" is not positivist. Marx is opposed to philosophical materialisms of all sorts, and pleads for one grounded in the "real interests" of humanity. Analogously, Laruelle is radically skeptical of positivism, as it is a form of philosophical construction of exactness rather than one determined by the real or by immanence. Positivism is a cosmology that amphibologically usurps the places of the real and of truth simultaneously, implying they are one and the same thing, and, hence, interchangeable. It is not mathematized, nor does it attempt to mathematize or quantify by performing a mimicry of scientific procedures that pertain to exact sciences. The sciences of or about humans, along with its method and possible formalization of language for the sake of exactitude, should be determined by the real in the last instance. The exactness of its language should issue from the "syntax of the real" (Laruelle) of subject matter in its study.

The real in non-standard Marxism—or in Marxism of non-philosophical posture of thought—is analogous to what Marx calls the worker's "interest."[3] The "syntax of the real" that Laruelle

---

[3] Karl Marx, "First Manuscript: Wages of Labor," in Karl Marx, *Economic and Philosophical Manuscripts of 1844* (Moscow: Progress Publishers, 1959), available at https://www.marxists.org/archive/marx/works/1844/manuscripts/wages.htm.

argues for in *Introduction au non-marxism* is dictated by what one would call "material reasons," or reasons originating from "the real," from the "physical," or from "life," according to Marx's *Capital*. It is important to note that in the first volume of *Capital*, contrary to the inertia of the doctrinal Marxian reading of the text, Marx resorts to the notions of "the real" and "life" virtually in all instances where we would expect to read "matter" or the "material." The legacy of Marxist interpretation—or simply, the legacy of "Marxism"—has introduced a doctrine of reading the original text by automatically and surreptitiously "translating" or interchanging the terms "life," "real," and "physical," with "matter." The idea of "materialism" has disciplined all possible readings of the concepts at issue.

The direct "interest" of the workers that Marx writes about is not an idea in the sense of "causa finalis." It's not a purpose. It does not have a "meaning" per se. It does not require "wisdom," "superior knowledge," or education to know what one's interest is. Interest is experienced, it is lived and it is the derivate of—let us put it in Spinozian terms, the conatus to stay in life and to increase lifepower. Through physical experience and mental representation or transposition, one knows what one's interest is. Philosophy, understood in Laruellian as well as in a Marxian sense, can drive us into violating our own interests by way of replacing the real (of life) with "truth." In Marxian terms, "fetishism" (and not only over commodities) can lead us to violate our immediate needs for a fulfilled life, which consists of a general state of physical and mental wellbeing, driving us into becoming (aspiring) capitalists. Not much different from this aspiration is the one that conditioned the establishment of the so-called communist societies, which Marx anticipated in his *Philosophic-Economic Manuscripts* in 1844 under the name of "primitive form of communism." It is an aspiration of a community and it is defined by its tendency of becoming a "universal capitalist."[4]

I.2. THE FETISH

The interest (Marx) or the lived (Laruelle) necessitates a response that seeks to protect the physical from the violence brought upon it

---

[4] Karl Marx, "Third Manuscript," in *Marx, Economic and Philosophical Manuscripts of 1844* (available at http://www.marxists.org/archive/marx/works/1844/manuscripts/third.htm): "The community is only a community of *labour*, and equality of wages paid out by communal capital—by the *community* as the universal capitalist. Both sides of the relationship are raised to an *imagined* universality—labour as the category in which every person is placed, and *capital* as the acknowledged universality and power of the community."

in the name—or by the dictate—of the "fetish." In Marx's text, "the fetish" equals the value of an absolute of an Idea/l, be it religious or political. The response of the real (of "the interest" that is material, physical, or of "the lived") is always already political, as it is one of either submission or rebellion. It is shaped by what Laruelle calls "the syntax of the real," by virtue of being conditioned by either the physical or by some life-protecting necessity that is in the last instance physical.

The real unavoidably seeks to be protected from the speculations of fetishism. The philosophical doubles the instances and oppositions that they create, i.e. matter and idea. Marxism understood as a philosophical project aims to reclaim the real identified with matter and emancipate it from the dictate of the idea or of the speculative. Building on Marx's texts, Marxism is a materialist philosophical project. The ambitions of Marx's texts, including the *Economic and Philosophical Manuscripts of 1844* and *Capital*, are minimally philosophical. They are characterized by the tendency to constitute a science in its own right, a science that is determined by its ambition to do away with philosophy. Laruelle's own project is founded on the exact same objective. Nonetheless, its defining specificities make of it a project that builds, albeit not solely, on some of Marx's own commitments. Both projects are by proclamation scientific, but not so in the sense of mannerist mimicry of exact sciences. They are scientific in the sense that they are the result of an exhaustive and systematic description of processes that are an inalienable and constitutive part of an experienced, i.e., "physical" or "sensuous," reality. For a human reality to be real, or to constitute a certain real for the subject of knowledge, it has to hold the status of an exteriority with respect to the thought that seeks to explain it.

To consider a reality subject to theoretical or scientific investigation as "objective" means to ascribe to it a meaning and to subject it to that meaning—to conflate it with it, and reduce it to it. The same goes for "material," as materialism is still a philosophical project, in spite of Marx's attempt to create a materialist science beyond or outside of philosophy. Positivism and materialism equate truth with reality; through this equation it establishes a neutralization of the real by instituting the "truth" of it as a higher form of reality. Such tendencies resemble the infantile mimetic impulse of creating a real that is more real than the real itself. According to Laruelle, science is defined precisely by it not being "spontaneous." The argument of the "human-in-human" in non-philosophy, or how the human in the last instance is marked by its linguistic insufficiency, implies that there is a continuity between common sense, or everyday man's and woman's language, and that of science. "Human-in-human" (homme-en-homme) refers to the kernel of the real in the human that precedes the lingual and the subjectivization as the product of language (or transcendence, in non-philosophical vocabulary). This concept has been elaborated in a most detailed way in Laruelle's *Théorie des Etrangers: Science des hommes, démocratie et non-psychanalyse* (1995).[5]

Nonetheless, science is defined by the break from the "human-in-human," while it remains on the same continuum of signification.

I.3. The Question of "Philosophical Amphibology"

Science, in the sense of non-philosophy or non-standard philosophy, is a method conditioned by the object of study that is a "real object." Being an "object"—albeit "real" as in "affected by immanence"—it is fundamentally a postulation. It is a quadruple postulation of "reality, exteriority, stability and unity," writes Laruelle.[6] Also, non-philosophically speaking, the object of scientific study is necessarily a *one* even when the final goal is to explain a complexity consisting of multiple elements. It is exterior to thought because it cannot be subsumed by it, and doesn't relate to it in any way in spite of the fact that thought unilaterally relates to the object of study. It is "stable," since what one scientifically seeks to explain is an identity in the last instance.[7] In this way, thought establishes a non-circular relation with the Real, without a reciprocal determination, which causes that cognition subjects itself to the real, rather than the other way around.[8] A rigor in description is what characterizes science's elimination of any auto-referentiality, explains Laruelle in *Intoduction au non-marxisme*. A scientific description of scientific praxis then, as Laruelle undertakes in *Théorie des identités*, presents us with the quadruple postulation of an object of scientific investigation. The descriptiveness of science is determined by its ambition to identify and explain the effects of the real, or what could be termed empiric processes, without empiricism. Scientific postures of thought seek to describe with language that which is exterior to language, without being encumbered with the pretensions to stipulate a universe of meaning. This permits the possibility of a radical fragmentation of knowledge. To stipulate and institute a universe of meaning is the characteristic of the philosophical mode of thinking. This means that they are characteristic of any

---

[5] François Laruelle, *Théorie des Etrangers: Science des hommes, démocratie et non-psychanalyse* (Paris: Éditions Kimé, 1995).
[6] François Laruelle, *Théorie des identités* (Paris: Presses Universitaires de France, 1992), 92.
[7] Laruelle, *Théorie des identités*, 92-93.
[8] François Laruelle, *Introduction au non-marxisme* (Paris: Presses Universitaires de France, 2000).

philosophy because they are the determination in the last instance of the philosophical.

I.4. Laruelle's "Scientific"

The objections directed against Laruelle's alleged generalization or reductionism of philosophy, when he speaks of 'philosophy' as if it were a monolithic and fixed phenomenon, are based on the claim that philosophy is essentially heterogeneous and diverse. This claim about philosophy's essential heterogeneity implies that there is a generic determination of philosophy. It implies there is a criterion according to which different teachings and writings in different historical periods can be named or identified as "philosophy." Laruelle's claim about philosophy's sufficiency and its immanent tendency for establishing circular relation with reality is his criterion for placing forms of thought and writing under the category of "philosophy." Since, according to Laruelle, the amphibology of thought, the real, and thought's self-sufficiency determine philosophy in the last instance, one can speak of philosophy in a scientific theory or a theological doctrine, but not necessarily of the philosophy canonically identified as such.

Consequently, Laruelle's reference to "the philosophy" is not a generalization of something that has been identified as philosophy according to criteria other those inherent to the non-philosophy. "The philosophy," according to non-philosophy, is anything whose determination in the last instance is a circular reciprocity between thought and the real, whereby the latter undergoes subsumption by the former. Scientific method is defined by terms that are themselves non-philosophical, and is affected and determined in the last instance by the praxis of science. It is according to this definition, without any reference to the philosophy of science or epistemology, which I shall refer to the notion of the scientific. Also, my identification of Marx's method in *Capital* as scientific is established according to the non-philosophical conceptualization of the scientific—not according to the doctrine of dialectical materialism or any other philosophical doctrine. I believe this usage of the term coincides with Marx's own understanding of the notion of "science" as determined by praxis rather than philosophy or "abstraction."

I.5. Marx's "Scientific"

Marx's method, conditioned by "the real," corresponds with the concept of a "real object" in non-standard philosophy, in that it identifies, describes, and explains the social-economic foundations of capitalism and the laws of functioning of the capitalist reality. On the basis of this acquired knowledge, a political vision is created. It is a vision that seeks to abolish subjection produced through alienation. The alienation at issue is (at least) threefold: one is alienated from one's labor, one is alienated from the fruits of one's labor, and finally, one is alienated from the physicality of one's life by subjecting them to the rule of an idea.

Following Laruelle, let us observe the syntax of the real as conditioned by the posture of thought which observes, describes, and explains the effects-in-the-real of the material reality of such alienation. By following the effects of the real on a thinking subject, this posture of thought carries out a rigorous description, thereby constituting a syntax of the real. Only thereafter does the non-philosophical or scientific posture of thought resort to the morphology and semantics originating in the "transcendental material" (language and philosophical concepts). In this manner, the source of the problem (i.e. of alienation) is explained, and a solution to it is presented. The proposed solution assumes the form of a response to the raised problem, a response that consists of the attempt to invent societal and economic models that would abolish or radically diminish the alienation in question. It stems from the problem of surplus value.

Surplus value is what grounds capitalist logic and enables its progressive, and ultimately out of joint, detachment from the material/real embodied by the sense and experience of need, termed by Marx as "interest."[9] This exchange, which is in its last instance a circular movement where money is exchanged for more money, is expressed in the formula M-C-M—the axiom of Marx's *Capital*. M-C-M establishes an endless cycle that takes on a life of its own. It exploits that which has use value: material objects that are turned into a commodity, or any object of human labor or nature that serves the needs for survival and a "spiritually and physically" fulfilled life.

> With this division of labour on the one hand and the accumulation of capital on the other, the worker becomes ever more exclusively dependent on labour, and on a particular, very one-sided, machine-like labour at that. Just as he is thus depressed spiritually and physically to the condition of a machine and from being a man becomes an abstract activity and a belly, so he also becomes ever more dependent on every fluctuation in market price.[10]

Commodification of labor drives any subject to the logic of M-C-M (not only the exploited, but also the exploiter) to a greater

---

[10] Marx, "First Manuscript: Wages of Labor," in *Marx, Economic and Philosophical Manuscripts of 1844*.
[11] Marx, "First Manuscript," in *Marx, Economic and Philosophical Manuscripts of 1844*.

alienation from the reality of her/his life as "sensuous" (Marx). Alienation or abstraction, which Marx identifies as the main source (or perhaps, the essence itself) of exploitation is not the same as transcendence in non-philosophy.

I.6. Transcendence, Alienation and Philosophically Impoverished Metaphysics

Marx argues that transcendence of the bare reality of a wage laborer's life, of the vulnerable exposure to exploitation of a life reduced to labor force, is the main goal of human economic and social emancipation. Let us consider the following quote from Marx's Economic and Philosophic Manuscripts 1844:

> Communism as the positive transcendence of private property as human self-estrangement, and therefore as the real appropriation of the human essence by and for man; communism therefore as the complete return of man to himself as a social (i.e., human) being—a return accomplished consciously and embracing the entire wealth of previous development. This communism, as fully developed naturalism, equals humanism, and as fully developed humanism equals naturalism; it is the genuine resolution of the conflict between man and nature and between man and man—the true resolution of the strife between existence and essence, between objectification and self-confirmation, between freedom and necessity, between the individual and the species. Communism is the riddle of history solved, and it knows itself to be this solution.[11]

This indicates that the communist project is not just about economic emancipation of the "human species" from its objectification as a labor force. Its goal is, evidently, also metaphysical, as communism is the "genuine resolution of the conflict between man and nature and between man and man," accomplished through "transcendence of [...] human estrangement."

The goal of transcending the alienation of man from nature is metaphysical, since its concern is one involving the reconciliation of realities that depend on a reconciliation of concepts. Although the concepts at stake are philosophical categories—that is to say, they are presented to us philosophically, either through theology or through the political theology of modernity—the goal consists in transcending philosophy. Therefore, what we will term here

---

[12] Marx, "Third Manuscript," in *Marx, Economic and Philosophical Manuscripts of 1844*.

"the metaphysical goal of Marxism" (or of Marxist communism and socialism), is in fact a "transcendentally impoverished metaphysics." The procedure of "transcendental impoverishment" is developed as part of Laruelle's non-philosophical method of theorizing with "philosophical material" by ridding its concepts of the philosophical principles of sufficiency.

> This is its [philosophy's] fundamental autopositioning, that which one could also call its autofactualization or its autofetishization—all that we assemble under the principle of sufficient philosophy (PPS).[12]

Marx argues that "alienation" is the product of philosophy, or the product of abstraction's domination and silencing of the "physical and sensuous" (the real and praxis). Thus, his project decidedly consists in transcending or exiting philosophy.[13] However, the proposal for the reconciliation of the mutually estranged notions and realities of "nature" and "man" posits questions as overwhelming as *why is the universe created* and as stubborn as *why is there death*, or *is there a God*? These questions are not necessarily philosophical. They are, nonetheless, metaphysical. They might be scientifically or logically meaningless, but this does not make them less relevant or meaningless. They can be addressed through religion but also through psychoanalysis. Also, I would argue, they can be tackled realistically from a certain point with the "science of the humans" that Laruelle seeks to establish, which can be constructed with the "transcendental material" of philosophy while remaining in the last instance determined by the real. In his *Introduction au Non-Marxisme*, Laruelle proposes the model for such science:

> If it [non-Marxism] would seem to go back there [to Marxism], it would be more to its problems rather than to its texts, and to problems whose solution implies treating the texts as symptoms, by way of suspension of the philosophical authority. [...] It is impossible, even in Freud and in Marx, and even more so within a philosophy, to find radical concepts of the Real and the universal—solely the unconscious and the productive forces, desire and labor. As soon as one arrives to this discovery, psychoanalysis and Marxism gain one utterly new sense—a transformation of their theories into simple material [...] These sorts of disciplines

---

[13] François Laruelle, *Philosophie et non-philosophie* (Liege: Pierre Mardaga, 1989), 17.
[14] Karl Marx, "Third Manuscript: Private Property and Communism," in Marx, *Economic and Philosophical Manuscripts of 1844*, available at https://www.marxists.org/archive/marx/works/1844/manuscripts/comm.htm.

require more than just a simple theoretical transformation—a discovery from within a "non-" that would be the effect (of) the Real or its action.[14]

The metaphysical questions raised in Marx's texts can be tackled through a posture of thought that is informed by the materialist tendency of transcending philosophy, a task Marx set for himself and for socialism. In its ambitions, Marx's materialism is fundamentally non-philosophical, as we can learn from his *Theses on Feuerbach*[15] and *Critique of Hegel's Philosophy in General.*[16]

Estrangement is seen as the material fact of alienation of the worker from his or her work: it is a process that does not belong to him or her. Hence, there is absence of a sense of familiarity. Not belonging to what one is most engaged to, the impossibility to claim this process as one's own labor (insofar it is waged) causes a sense of radical estrangement that is experienced as suffering of the body and soul.

Not being at home with one's own immediate and constant activity, a state expressed primarily through the status of "a worker," is as painful as it is dispossessing to one's sense of selfhood. This is a form of violence that is specific to humankind. Marx's communism is essentially a humanist project. For the same reason, Laruelle declares his project of non-philosophy as one of "the sciences of the human." Let us note, Marx and Laruelle's humanism is not philosophical as they are seen respectively as scientific projects based on the gesture of "an exit from philosophy" (Marx) or a stance of a "non" with respect to philosophy that steps out from "philosophy's sufficiency" (Laruelle).

Marx insists on the communist model or goal of liberation as one founded in the "real," "physical," or "natural" experience of estrangement. The estrangement Marx writes about is not the same as the estrangement that existentialists have written about, as it does not deal with the question of meaning or meaninglessness of life. It does not discover the "absurd" as simultaneously the real and the truth of human existence, or estrangement as its essence. Quite to the contrary, estrangement is far from being the essence of human existence; it is what deprives humanity from "realization" of its essence that is rooted in the "physical," "natural," and "the

---

[15] François Laruelle, *Introduction au non-marxisme* (Paris: Presses Universitaires de France, 2000), 61.
[16] Marx, "Theses on Feuerbach," in Marx and Engels, *The German Ideology*.
[17] Karl Marx, "Critique of Hegel's Philosophy in General," in Marx, *Economic and Philosophical Manuscripts of 1844*, available at https://www.marxists.org/archive/marx/works/1844/manuscripts/hegel.htm..

real." Estrangement is experienced or lived—in Laruellian terms it is the instance of the lived (*le vecu*)—as trauma, and is a form of oppression by virtue of the sheer experience of inflicted violence and pain that it causes to the human "body" and "spirit."

II. Commodity Fetishism and the Speculative Mind as Two Faces of the Same Mode of Oppression and Exploitation

II.1. Alienation of Labor through Abstraction

> The value of commodities is the very opposite of the coarse materiality of their substance, not an atom of matter enters into its composition.
>
> –Karl Marx, *Capital*

Marx unmasks the complete lack of materiality as the condition for determination in the last instance of commodity qua commodity. The product of human labor assumes the status of a commodity only when it is absolutely detached from its physicality.

> There is a physical relation between physical things. But it is different with commodities. There, the existence of the things quâ commodities, and the value relation between the products of labour which stamps them as commodities, have absolutely no connection with their physical properties and with the material relations arising. [17]

The production and exchange of commodities is grounded in an estrangement from the physical. The estrangement first takes place in the form of the exploitation of human labor as physicality, and in a second gesture, by way of entering the endless (or circular) chain of exchange of values, it assumes the status of a commodity. Abstraction as the determination in the last instance of all commodities, and of the circulation of the commodity as (surplus) pure value is enabled by the exploitation of human labor, which, in its turn, is always physical.

> The mystical character of commodities does not originate, therefore, in their use value. Just as little does it proceed from the nature of the determining factors of value. For, in

---

[18] Karl Marx, "The Fetishism of Commodities and the Secret Thereof," in Karl Marx, *Capital: A Critique of Political Economy*, Vol. I: The Process of Production of Capital, ed. Frederick Engels, trans. Samuel Moore and Edward Aveling (Moscow: Progress Publishers, 1887), available at http://www.marxists.org/archive/marx/works/1867-c1/ch01.htm#S4.

the first place, however varied the useful kinds of labour, or productive activities, may be, it is a physiological fact, that they are functions of the human organism, and that each such function, whatever may be its nature or form, is essentially the expenditure of human brain, nerves, muscles, &c.[18]

It seems that exploitation is in essence unavoidably fetishistic, as it is the effect of abstraction directed against the physical. Immediate needs that are expressed in and satisfied through the so-called use-value of a product are in the last instance physical, especially when they primarily concern the "mind" (or brain and nerves). Only if these physical needs are sacrificed, and if they become subject to the holocaust of speculation (economic but also philosophical), is commodity created, and with it the possibility of surplus value.

A close reading of most of Marx's seminal texts disclose a repeated and consistent stance, according to which exploitation is always already carried out by the instance of the speculative and the abstract against the physical, or the real or material (all three terms are used by Marx interchangeably). This argument is the core of his critique of fetishism. It is also, I would argue, the grounding epistemic position of his entire oeuvre. All questions that do not depart from the real of existence, or simply from the lived, are ill posed and lead toward speculation based on the procedure of abstraction.

> Your question is itself a product of abstraction. Ask yourself how you arrived at that question. Ask yourself whether your question is not posed from a standpoint to which I cannot reply, because it is wrongly put. Ask yourself whether that progress as such exists for a reasonable mind. When you ask about the creation of nature and man, you are abstracting, in so doing, from man and nature. You postulate them as non-existent, and yet you want me to prove them to you as existing. Now I say to you: Give up your abstraction and you will also give up your question.[19]

The "material" that Marx invokes as the authority in the last instance of every operation of thought, which seeks to establish accurate knowledge about the reality, is "material" insofar as it is "physical," "sensuous," and "real." It is unequivocally stated so in

---

[19] Marx, "The Fetishism of Commodities and the Secret Thereof," in Marx, *Capital*, Vol. 1.
[20] Marx, "Third Manuscript," in Marx, *Economic and Philosophical Manuscripts of 1844*.

Marx's first thesis on Feuerbach:

> The chief defect of all hitherto existing materialism—that of Feuerbach included—is that the thing, reality, sensuousness, is conceived only in the form of the object or of contemplation, but not as a sensuous human activity, practice, not subjectively. Hence, in contradistinction to materialism, the active side was developed abstractly by idealism—which, of course, does not know real, sensuous activity as such.[20]

Human activity, particularly human subjectivity, is not reducible to physical activity. In the above quote Marx resorts to such terms as "the thing," "reality," and "practice," as different names for the same referent. Physicality only vouches that the object of cognition is not an abstraction: that it is anchored in the real.

II.2. The Status of Materialism in Marx's Realism

Marx unequivocally states in his *Theses on Feuerbach* that he does not place materialism as an idea in the history of philosophy. What Marx argues for is a particular kind of materialism that is not philosophical, the product of operations of abstraction, or one that is detached or oppositional to the physical. Rather, he strives to create a science of humanity's "species-being" that is determined in the last instance by the immediacy of an experienced reality. Countering and transcending the experience of suffering caused by alienation (the latter being caused by abstraction) is the goal that Marx's political project seeks to attain. Materialism is merely a form of realism for Marx; he argues it only insofar as it departs from "the thing"[21] and the "sensuous human activity, practice."[22] The antithesis between matter and idea here is also one imposed by abstract contemplation. The goal of humanity then, according to Marx, should be emancipation from all forms of oppression and subjugation. This depends on the abolishment of antitheses established by the "abstract" or "false consciousness." It can be accomplished by rooting thought in practice, or in the real.

We see how subjectivity and objectivity, spirituality and

---

[21] Marx, "Theses on Feuerbach," in Marx and Engels, *The German Idealism*.
[22] Marx, "Third Manuscript: Private Property and Communism," in Marx, *Economic and Philosophical Manuscripts of 1844*.
[23] Marx, "Theses on Feuerbach," in Marx and Engels, *The German Idealism*.

> materiality, activity and suffering, lose their antithetical character, and—thus their existence as such antitheses only within the framework of society; we see how the resolution of the theoretical antitheses is only possible in a practical way, by virtue of the practical energy of man. Their resolution is therefore by no means merely a problem of understanding, but a real problem of life, which philosophy could not solve precisely because it conceived this problem as merely a theoretical one.[23]

The chief concern of Marxism is ensuring realism, for thought and the body, rather than materialism. Transcending intra-individual and inter-individual alienation is—Marx puts very explicitly—about abolishing the opposition between "spirituality" and "materiality." The opposition itself—for the "antithesis"—is "merely a theoretical one." The use of the "theoretical" here has the same function as that of "philosophy" in Laruelle's non-standard philosophy. This binary logic, which is defined by the opposition between an instance that only can be a product of cognitive operation, and an instance that is a cognitive product nonetheless, is determined by the real and only can be the product of philosophy. In other words, the postulation of "the Idea" or "the Spirit," and the postulation of its opposite, i.e., "the matter" or "materiality," is the result of philosophical reasoning that is determined in the last instance by "theory" rather than practice or the real.

II.3. Marx's Theory and Laruelle's Philosophy

In non-standard philosophy, the term "theory" refers to thought's transcendental substratum, which can be rid of philosophy or of the authority of philosophy through determination in the last instance of a purported truth. There is a perfect parallel between Marx's use of "theory," for which he also often uses synonyms like "philosophy," "abstraction," and "speculation," and Laruelle's use of the term "philosophy." Marx argues for a materialism that will not be philosophical in the last instance, but rather one that will cause the meaning of the term to vanish.

> [...] we see how consistent naturalism or humanism is distinct from both idealism and materialism, and constitutes at the same time the unifying truth of both. We see also how only naturalism is capable of comprehending

---

[24] Marx, "Third Manuscript," in Marx, *Economic and Philosophical Manuscripts of 1844*.

the action of world history.[24]

The disappearance of the term will be the product of the abolishing of the opposition that determines it. The opposition will be "abolished" by the submission of both terms to the authority of the real, which determines each of them in their own right as instances of the real. "Spirituality," or a "spiritually fulfilled life," is the goal of the socialist and communist idea, writes Marx. Thus it is spirituality that is experienced, lived, and materialized as sensuous or real. Hence, its opposition to the material is obsolete. Marx explains that socialism or communism seeks to reverse this reality:

> With this division of labour on the one hand and the accumulation of capital on the other, the worker becomes ever more exclusively dependent on labour, and on a particular, very one-sided, machine-like labour at that. Just as he is thus depressed spiritually and physically [my emphasis] to the condition of a machine and from being a man becomes an abstract activity and a belly, so he also becomes ever more dependent on every fluctuation in market price, on the application of capital, and on the whim of the rich.[25]

The "spiritual depression" only can be overcome by transcending and abolishing the human's "condition of a machine," which happens when someone or something becomes "an abstract activity and a belly." Spiritually and physically exuberant life is possible only if ideas are a part of and made from human praxis, forming a sense of "being real" and making one "feel real" and integral (without the division between "abstract activity and a belly"). Realistically (in the materialist mode according to Marx), a postulated question or concept is determined unilaterally by one instance—the instance of the real.

II.4. THE REAL OF JOY AND SUFFERING ACCORDING TO MARX AND LARUELLE

Enjoyment and suffering no longer establish opposition. They are both instances of the lived, of the sheer experience that takes place as "suffering," in the etymological sense of the Latin word passio. One is subjected to a sensation, be it pleasure or pain, which takes

---

[25] Marx, "Critique of Hegel's Philosophy in General," in Marx, *Economic and Philosophical Manuscripts of 1844*.
[26] Marx, "First Manuscript," in Marx, *Economic and Philosophical Manuscripts of 1844*.

place in the defenseless body through the instance of pure exposure and vulnerability. Similarly, Laruelle's "the lived" is called *le joui*, regardless of whether it is the product of the infliction of pain or pleasure. "It is the undivided (of) pain—yet not determined by it—as the undivided lived of joy, but never their synthesis, not even immanent."[26] The unilateral, mute instance of the lived in Marx's text is called suffering, regardless of whether it is the result of violence or a sensation of pleasure.

> [...] the object is the *manifestation of the human reality*, [...] it is human *activity* and human *suffering*, for suffering, humanly considered, is a kind of self-enjoyment of man.[27]

Suffering is self-enjoyment, not because of some vague masochistic inclination, but because it represents a surpassed alienation. Pain situates us in the real of ourselves. The real is the instance one inhabits prior to any "making sense out of it"—in anteriority vis-à-vis language—it precedes any possibility of abstraction (including that of "abstract activity and a belly"). Laruelle's "joui sans jouissance" is one of the "first names" of the real that we all are in the last instance.[28] It is the enjoyed, without the idea of "enjoyment," without conceptualization or a philosophy of enjoyment, without attaching it any sort of value.

That invasion of sensation, whether undergone as pain or pleasure, is suffering since it entails unmitigated exposure. Without the subject of language that transforms it into representation, phantasm, or idea/l, it is helpless passivity. Nonetheless, if the lingual subject introduces abstraction to the extent of causing a sense of estrangement from the real that we are, or the bundle of sensations that each of are in the last instance, we are subjugated and repressed, since we are detached from our most immediate physical needs. Abstraction or self-subjugation by philosophy is the only means through which we can become accomplices in our own subjugation from others.

According to Laruelle's non-standard psychoanalysis operating with the "transcendental material" of Lacan's psychoanalysis— the instance of the "Stranger" (or the process of estrangement as pre-subjectivization) is unavoidable and necessary in order to mediate the traumatic immediacy of the real. Laruelle says "The Strangers are radical subjectivities", rather than "persons, individuals or subjects in the technical transcendental sense of the

---

[27] Laruelle, *Théorie des Etrangers*, 225.
[28] Marx, "Third Manuscript," in Marx, *Economic and Philosophical Manuscripts of 1844*.
[29] Laruelle, *Théorie des Etrangers*, 222.

word."[29] Laruelle's Stranger is made of "transcendental material" since it is a form of subjectivity, or the product of language (regardless of how transcendentally minimal). Nonetheless, it also is radical since it is experienced as a "point of exteriority" at the heart of the real. Unlike Lacan's barred Subject, the radical subjectivity viz. the Stranger, (as defined by Laruelle), possesses a "concrete body" or "flesh," one consisting of the "multitudes of transcendental material."[30] Thus, the experience of estrangement, which is an instance of suffering that takes place through the real that we are, must not be erased through a double abstraction— i.e. an abstraction of and alienation from the pre-subjective and the founding experience of estrangement (of subjectivity). The process of alienation from the immediacy of the real—through the instance of the Stranger or radical subjectivity—introduces the trauma of the foundational split. The pain of that unavoidable split is inalienable; it takes place in or as the real.

If recognized as a dyad that is constituted by thought's unilateral position with respect to the real and by the indifferent (to thought) unilaterality of the real, and if this dyad is radically determined as such, the instance of alienation remains an exteriority. To radically determine the dyad as such and think it and its constitutive elements in terms of this radicalization is to perform an act of dualysis, which is the founding methodological gesture of non-philosophy and/or non-standard philosophy. In that way, thought is not collapsed into and surreptitiously identified with the real of the pain that is caused by the experience of auto-alienation viz. the primordial split. Dualysis, in Laruelle's terminology, is a procedure of unilateral affirmation of the dyad.[31] The non-abstractionist (or non-philosophical) recognition of the grounding alienation of the Self should affirm radical alienation without the gesture of self-mirroring that would produce its philosophical double.

II.5. Wage Labor as Abstraction or as the Product of Philosophy

The abstract value of a commodity or work as wage labor is the product of philosophical procedure. According to the logic of wage

---

[30] Laruelle, *Théorie des Etrangers*, 166 : "Concrètement les Etrangers ne sont pas des personnes, des individus ou des sujets au sens philosophique transcendant de ces mots; ce sont bien de toute façon des subjectivités radicales, mais en dernière instance; et ce qui leur tien lieu de corps—de corps transi par cette subjectivité—, est de l'ordre de ces entités sans différence et tissées dans la transcendance du vide."
[31] Laruelle, *Théorie des Etrangers*, 166: "On peut appeler 'chair' les Multitudes transcendantales=X … ."
[32] Laruelle, *Philosophie et non-philosophie*, 93–95.

labor, "meaning" and signification establish an amphibology with the real—they act in its stead while still pretending to re-present it—and in a subterfuge movement of thought establish absolute authority over it. This would be a Laruellian definition of "the philosophical." Unlike the pretensions of scientific thought that describe and explain the workings of an instance of the real, philosophy seeks to re-present the real with totality, without a remainder, to reflect it fully. However, the unruly real does not possess the qualities of a logically or metaphysically consistent system or doctrine. Therefore, instead of describing it and explaining it as an exteriority, philosophical thought engulfs the real either with the modern and pre-modern philosophical claim of total reflection of the real, or through the postmodern abolition of the real by its declaration as "obsolete." It is declared "obsolete" insofar as it is assigned the status of the "unthinkable" (in a Lacanian, deconstructivist, and postmodernist sense). Thus, the real is declared "meaningless," and as such, an irrelevant subject for social theory in the academically established disciplines of the humanities. How we construct the realities of our existence has become the only epistemologically relevant question in the era of poststructuralism.

II.6. Linguistic Realities are "An Out There" in the Financial and Philosophical Capitalism of Today

Following Marx's critique of alienation through abstraction and Laruelle's philosophically non-standard recuperation of the real, my claim is that the theoretical investigation of the modes of lingual construction of our realities should be conducted in a way so those realities are affirmed as exteriority (i.e., instances of the real in their own right). It is indispensible to do so in order to arrive to the possibility of overcoming the dictatorship of speculation in contemporary financial capitalism, postmodern theory, and politics (translated into concrete policies affecting the lives of concrete individuals).

The linguistic delineation of the horizon of political possibility establishes a conditional limit and defines the size and the topology of the politically thinkable. The delineated topos is not an instantiation of "the transcendental imagination" in Kantian sense. Quite on the contrary, it is an exteriority and an instance of the real because it is not the product of the autonomous and sovereign subject, but the deployment of a complex reality affected by the real of materiality and physicality (as an aspect of the social), which is by definition the product of a linguistically mediated real.

The real is not necessarily a physical exteriority. Rather, it is an exteriority that is outside the reach of our linguistic intervention, appropriation, and re-invention. The real is an effect that is experienced as violence (as the implacable limit to our signifying automatism), as a linguistically non-negotiable limitation, and as what Lacan would call the *tuché* that happens to the (signifying) automaton in the form of trauma. This instance is the concept of capital and the material and immaterial realities that it creates. The ideology of capitalism stipulates the possibility of any reality we can inhabit and imagine. Therefore, the exteriority that holds the status of the real is not necessarily physical. Moreover, the real is not necessarily exterior since it can be an internally experienced limit/ation to the subject's signifying pretensions.

2: The Possibility of Immanent Revolt as Theory and Political Praxis

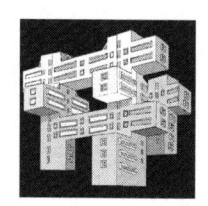

I. Immanence of Revolt

The only way to immanently revolt against the world is in the non-abstract. Revolting against concrete occurrences of subjugation and violence, rather than in the name of abstraction and in visions of world transformation, is political action affected by immanence. I would argue that immanence is also action determined by interests which are real and sensuous (or material), rather than abstract or philosophical. According to Marx, as discussed in the previous chapter, abstraction itself is what ought to be combated when one resists capitalism. A communist or Marxist socialist strives toward the creation of a world in consonance with the real or the material and immediate exigency. Laruelle would say that the world would always be made of philosophy, and that it would always already persecute the human in human (*l'homme-en-homme*). The permanent process of the democratic transformation of society, as envisaged by Marx, should be determined by real interests rather than abstraction. The goal would be that the world becomes a more just and happy place, one where persecution is minimalised by virtue of the reversed hierarchy between philosophy and the real, where the former would succumb to the dictate of the latter.

Revolt is immanent when it is determined in the last instance by the lived of revolt, not by acting as a transcendental moral or political decision or reacting against another moral or political vision. The experience of revolt void of philosophy precedes language—and therefore also transcendence. The revolt in question is not temporal, and its independence from the linguistic does not imply a metaphysically construed separate universe. The purely experiential or the lived revolt can be caused by the act of language which inflicts violence, whose reaction is rebellion that is an instantiation of conatus. As Spinoza expouds in *Ethics*, activity which increases life is the result of conatus, revolt, and the struggle that aims to maintain or intensify life by combating the life-decreasing activity of the body-mind suffered by an external or internal source of violence. Transforming violence into a law, into a "making sense" and the assumption of the position that accommodates the violence from one part of humanity over another, is what alienates one from suffering and joy. The function that enables the alienating operation of socio-economic repression is abstraction. Abstraction finds its purest form in capitalism—in the universe of pure speculation as the source of material domination and an absolute domination over the material.

The immanent rebellion that François Laruelle writes about consists in " the struggle without a goal," which is always already present in every human (not the human subject but the real of human, or in Laruelle's vocabulary, "the human-in-human"). It is without a goal because its only source and tendency is to protect itself from violence through alienation; this defense of the human-in-human is determined by radical vulnerability.

> [...] to struggle in an immanent way with the World, this is the theorem of the Future Christ. In the beginning was the struggle, and the struggle was with the World and the World did not know it [...] That is rebellion, its reasons and cause.[1]

Any political struggle that stems from the dictate of immanent rebellion is determined in this way. The struggle is one of radical singularity, but this does not mean that it cannot establish solidarity or that it is individualistic. On the contrary, it is pre-subjective whereas individualism presupposes subjectivity. The lived experience of vulnerability and struggle can be an experience of a collective, an experience that can be mute, pre-lingual, or radically solitary, insofar as it is only the witnesses of the experience that can communicate internally and according to the syntax of the real of what took place. The protestors of Istanbul in the summer of 2013 were faced with the challenge to formulate their political goals and convey the philosophical (or political) decision which determined their struggle, whereas the only truth they knew was "what took place" at Gezi park and the massive solidarity that it sparked. The

[1] François Laruelle, *Future Christ: A Lesson in Heresy*, trans. Anthony Paul Smith (London/New York: Continuum, 2010), 4.

brutality that Erdogan's government demonstrated was the reason for the demand that he leave office. Only then could the protestors define a political agenda that was still not philosophical—one determined not by ideology, but the concrete demands dictated by experienced reality. Revolt took place, struggle against institutionalized violence rose, and the sheer experience of revolt-struggle proffered the foundation which created a political agenda:

> In order to clarify the stakes and the limits of rebellion we pose the problem outside of philosophical bad habits. Philosophy is always indifferent to man or, though this isn't very different, too quickly compassionate. Sufferings and alienation exist in the necessity of revolt and one concludes from this that there is evil, and often evils, there too. Revolts are only 'logical' in this way—admirable vicious circle of uncertainty and the contingency of a desired rebellion in which no one believes.[2]

It is necessary that rebellion seems credible. Credibility implies planned steps toward achieving a goal that is determined by a philosophical decision (about "what and how the world should be"). The resistance to what inflicts subjugation is carried out from a vulnerable position by those who are determined in the last instance to be "persecuted."

> The theory of Future Christ makes of the being-murdered and the being-persecuted a universal but real criteria of the manifestation of Life rather than an absurd condition of historical fact.[3]

Life is conditioned by a sense of being persecuted, which brings forth immanence or the inevitability of revolt and struggle. Persecution is caused by "the world," which in Laruelle's terminology is analogous to philosophy—the universe of meaning.[4]

---

[2] Laruelle, *Future Christ*, 6.
[3] Laruelle, *Future Christ*, 6.
[4] The concept of the "world" as analogous to that of "philosophy" is developed throughout the entire opus of Laruelle. For the sake of illustration, let us consider the following quote from François Laruelle and Anne-Françoise Schmid's "L'identité sexuée," Identities : *Journal of Politics, Gender and Culture* 2.3 (2003) : 55: "Le problème du rapport des sexes au génie pourrait être également déplacé. Dans son interpretation 'philosophique' habituelle, il postule la capacité de vivre en son proper destin le destin du Monde et donc se jouer des contraires et de se les donner librement. C'est la faculté de se donner le Monde et le sentiment d'être pour lui plutôt qu'en lui. La-femme passe son énergie dans le Monde, puisqu'elle en assure la stabilité. Le Monde, dessiné par les structures de la philoso-

The universe of meaning is necessarily a universe of normality and orthodoxy. The immanent struggle or the human-in-human, determined by the immanence of struggle, is foundationally in revolt against orthodoxy and the world. The human-in-human in the last instance is a heretic. On the other hand, the world seeks to control him and her by subjugating them through abstraction that controls, moulds, violates the lived (*le vécu*, as Laruelle terms it), and acts in its stead.

II. THE WORLD AS PERSECUTION

> In human beings there is 'a something' of a radically outside-nature, and the World is a fundamental will that persecutes this heresy.
> - François Laruelle, *Future Christ*

Nature is part of the world, and thus is a creation of orthodoxy. Let us utilize Judith Butler's terminology in order to explain: Nature is always already a product of the imaginary, upon whose edifice norms and normality are erected. The immanent rebellion is rooted in humanity's realization of the lack of immanence in any norm, the norm's coercive ruse of posturing as a law of nature, and in the society that conforms with nature as the underlying truth of all existence. As Laruelle and Schmid put it,

> Man-in-person is not an empire within the empire of the World but is that from whom the Real takes precedent above those empires that persecute him and who, turning himself into a victim, confesses to his being-human in spite of them. By a decision of an axiomatic kind, we therefore place the protestations of rational sufficiency and the belief in philosophical and theological opinion between parentheses. We posit that the ethics of transcendence, as much as those of the immanence of the happy life, belong to the World, that the religions of the Book, just as the others, are religions of the death-World.[5]

Man-in-person, or subjectivity affected by immanence, is not a universe in its own right. The liberal myth of individual's sanc-

---

phie, peut être lui aussi transformé, en ce sens qu'il n'est pas nécessaire de se le donner dans son unité ni sa totalité. Il y faut une généralisation de la philosophie, sa transformation en matériau. Le génie pourrait alors apparaître sous des formes moins totalitaires et impulsives, moins masculines. C'est là aussi tout un travail de transformation des énoncés philosophiques, dont l'objet finit toujours par être quelque chose du Monde.
[5] Laruelle and Schmid, "L'identité sexuée," 19.

tity and its capacity to create a unique moral, political, esthetical universe—a "world"—is declared false. The only world we can be in, and the only world we represent, is the world in the sense of non-philosophy. The "world according to non-philosophy" is analogous to Lacan's symbolic order or Foucault's disciplining discourses of power. It is indeed formative of the subject, but the human in the last instance, according to Laruelle, is pre-subjective. It is the real of radical vulnerability and of the immanent revolting. The inexhaustible force of revolt is not based in philosophy or the world - it is situated in the radical opposition to it as it acts from the standpoint of the lived. The opposition to the world or the ruling norms/normativity is radically static. It is atemporal, and does not participate in the transformations of meaning the world produces. Nonetheless, it aspires to change the world in a way that will make it less brutal to the radical vulnerability that the human-in-human is. Immanent rebellion is static, both as "not moving" and in the Athenian political concept of *stasis* that means a rebellion or a civil war in the polis. Although stasis implies unrest, it remains static vis-à-vis the world and stops the endless signification that the world compulsively produces. It represents a suspension of the polis. Stasis, meaning both as stillness and revolution (στάσις), is a pause in the normality of the functioning state or world. Immanent revolt consists in the human-in-human's radical externality with respect to the unstoppable auto-generated processes of subjection (of "being a subject") in this world.

The world invades the mute lived (le vécu) of the human-in-human in the form of subjectivity. Meaning (sign), both general and abstract, aims to shape the real and produce joy and suffering according to the ruling forms of jouissance, which are philosophically determined. The *a priori* invasiveness of the world makes the human-in-human always already persecuted. The only way to immanently revolt against the world is in a non-abstract way. Revolting against concrete occurrences of subjugation and violence, rather than in the name of abstractions and visions of transformation of the world, is political action "affected by immanence."[6] It is also action determined by "interests" that are real and sensuous (or material), says Marx, rather than abstract or philosophical. As explained in the previous chapter, abstraction itself is what ought to be combated in order to create a world in consonance with the real or the material immediate exigency. As Laruelle would say, the world will be always made of philosophy and it will always already persecute the human-in-human. This constant revolution can transform it into a socio-political order which is observant of "real interests" rather than abstractions, writes Marx.

[6] François Laruelle, *Introduction au non-marxisme* (Paris: Presses Universitaires de France, 2000), 48.

III. To be a Victim and to be a Messiah: Radical Humanity

> The victim is defined by a radical passivity and not by an absolute one which Levinas attributes to the self. By definition, radical passivity cannot re-act through an excess of power or by overpowering, it is impossible for it to act in a reflexive manner, but it is capable of acting quite differently—by depotentializing philosophical overpowering.
>
> - François Laruelle, *Théorie générale des victimes*

Revolt can grow both immanently and infinitely—because infinity is dictated by intensity, and intensity is the mode of immanence—only if it undercuts philosophical pretension. Its power is passive since it is made of suffering. However, radical passivity is potent because it silences and cancels any philosophical decision regarding the suffering of the always already persecuted. Radical passivity, and the revolt it engenders, is a cry to all the masters of the world to cease their talk of victims and their liberation, to cease re-presenting them and alienating them through representation. Philosophical representation is never generic. It is an abstraction whose origin is purely transcendental, whereas the generic is a radical concept determined by the real and the "syntax of scientific description" that it dictates (see Laruelle's Introduction au non-marxisme). In *Théorie Générale des Victimes* (2012), Laruelle explains the notion of the "generic" in the context of the study of victims, and par consequence, both their revolt and the revolt of those who act in radical solidarity with them. "The generic," says Laruelle, "is a process of reduction of any philosophical or macroscopic entity, of its nature of a double, doubling, double transcendence (the consciences, the ego or a psycho-sociological identity). Reduction to a phenomenal immanence, one, however, lived as objective, subjected to the quantum principle of superposition is not a principle of a logical identity."[7] So, in the last instance, the identity of the victim should be defined as follows:

> In effect, the identity of the victim, if the latter is defined physically and generically, is of specific nature which builds on the proto-quantum procedure of superposition or interference, and in no way on psychological or social identification.[8]

---

[7] François Laruelle, *Théorie générale des victimes* (Paris: Fayard, 2012), 30.
[8] Laruelle, *Théorie générale des victimes*, 30: "L'identité de la victime en effet, si elle doit être définie physiquement et génériquement, est d'une nature spéciale qui appelle des procédure proto-quantique de superposition ou d'interférence, nullement d'identification psychologique ou sociale."

If we rid the concept of the victim of all its philosophical "essences," or all forms of representation which transform the lived suffering of the victims into pure transcendence (meanings of victimhood), we do away with the representation and the images (produced through media) of the victims which act in the stead of the victim's reality. The philosophically mediated idea of a victim, which is produced by the media and the intellectuals who represent and defend them, pretends to be the reality of the victims' suffering that is interpellated to identify with these images and the meanings that are assigned to them. Considering that the notions of the world and philosophy are synonymous in non-standard philosophy, the media is one of the most powerful and active machines of the production of philosophical images (or of the ruling representations in and of the world that dictates our actions). The more they seek to be realistic the more detached from the real they are. They establish, in Laruellian terms, an amphibology of the real and the philosophical (or the transcendental), whereby the latter acts instead of the former. The absurd is produced by the pretension that the "meaningful real" is more real than "just the real," with the latter being deemed as the unruly effect of "meaningless" thrust on an almost physical symptom—*tuché* as Lacan would call it—into the universe of meaning.

In *Théorie générale des victimes*, Laruelle invites us to establish a process of compassion (in its etymological sense) or co-suffering with the victim with a complete disregard for the mediation of victimhood by intellectuals (and their world of the media). How do we accomplish this goal?

If we reduce the humanist human to a human without humanism, or the instance of the real made of the lived of suffering (and joy), then what we are faced with in a victim in the last instance is the lived of suffering. To establish solidarity is to co-suffer by virtue of the rudimentary cognitive procedure of identification with the pain to which the other is subjected. Let us paraphrase Spinoza: one imagines the pain suffered by the other in a unilateral way; the pain invades the "imagination" of the co-sufferer that produces a "life-decreasing" effect.[9] One imagines the fundamental vulnerability of the other and of oneself, which is a procedure of Spinozian identification. The process of abstraction (cognitive and metaphysical/existential) only can enable alienation from the other persons's suffering, and thus fails to identify with its experience, viz. "imagine" with "life decreasing" effects. On the other hand, the tendency to establish compassion with what it means to be a victim, or what it means to suffer "the loss of dignity" and "value of the human life," is essentially philosophical. It always already

---

[9] Benedict de Spinoza, *The Ethics*, trans. by R. H. M. Elwes (The Project Gutenberg Etext Publication: 2003), III 30p.

alienates the real, which is the human in the last instance. Co-suffering with the other's real in terms of the real implies an abandonment of (philosophical) humanism. It produces a radically human sociality, or in Marx's terms, one in accordance with the interests of the "species being of humanity" rather than abstract ideas of general humanity.[10] Solidarity stems not solely from lived co-suffering, but also from the concomitant experience of immanent revolt or "immanent struggle" (Laruelle). Therefore, it is the lived of immanent revolt for the other's suffering as one's own which is the basis of solidarity—or rather, radical solidarity—in and for the "species" or "non-human" (the human without humanism).

Suffering immanently produces revolt, whereas co-suffering gives rise to an immanent revolt-in-species or radical solidarity (of the "non-human"). I would argue that revolt-in-species is determined by Marx's concept of the human species as a hybrid of socio-political relations (forming a whole), nature, and physiology. This is an idea of the human as a social and biological factum, without the abstractions of humanism. Therefore, the solidarity we establish with another human being, understood through a Marxian reading of Laruelle, is determined by biology as much as it is determined by the whole of heterogeneous and complex social relations. It is not driven by the idea of an essence of humanity that is incarnated by each human being.

> Feuerbach resolves the essence of religion into the essence of man [menschliche Wesen = 'human nature']. But the essence of man is no abstraction inherent in each single individual. In reality, it is the ensemble of the social relations.[11]

The human species is defined as an animal species, and is therefore determined in the last instance by nature:

> That man's physical and spiritual life is linked to nature means simply that nature is linked to itself, for man is a part of nature.[12]

---

[10] Karl Marx, *Economic and Philosophical Manuscripts of 1844* (Moscow: Progress Publishers, 1959), available at https://www.marxists.org/archive/marx/works/1844/manuscripts/preface.htm; Karl Marx, "Theses on Feuerbach," in Karl Marx and Frederick Engels, The German Ideology, trans. Roy Pascal (London: Lawrence and Wishart, 1938), available at http://www.marxists.org/archive/marx/works/1845/theses/.
[11] Marx, "Theses on Feuerbach," in Marx and Engels, *The German Ideology*.
[12] Karl Marx, "First Manuscript: Estranged Labor," in Marx, *Economic and Philosophical Manuscripts of 1844*, available at http://www.marxists.org/archive/marx/works/1844/manuscripts/labour.htm.

Solidarity is radically grounded in physicality. Namely, alienation—through objectification of labor—deprives the human being of their labor and of means of subsistence provided by nature, therefore subjugating them by virtue of rendering them first a worker and then as a physical subject. Political solidarity and collective revolt are, in the last instance, about overcoming the alienation of the human animal from nature as the source in the last instance of its means of subsistence, and as the real universe of their labor. It is also about overcoming alienation from and within the human universe of social and political relations. This process is also a return to the real, the material (without materialism), and the "sensuous" (Marx) human life and its relations to other beings, nature, and the products of labor as part of or non-alienated from nature:

> *Man* is directly a *natural being*. As a natural being and as a living natural being he is on the one; hand endowed with *natural powers*, *vital powers*—he is an *active* natural being. These forces exist in him as tendencies and abilities—as instincts. On the other hand, as a natural, corporeal, sensuous objective being he is a *suffering*, conditioned and limited creature, like animals and plants. That is to say, the *objects* of his instincts exist outside him, as objects independent of him; yet these objects are *objects* that he *needs*—essential objects, indispensable to the manifestation and confirmation of his essential powers. To say that man is a *corporeal*, living, real, sensuous, objective being full of natural vigour is to say that he has real, sensuous objects as the object of his being or of his life, or that he can only *express* his life in real, sensuous objects. To be objective, natural and sensuous, and at the same time to have object, nature and sense outside oneself, or oneself to be object, nature and sense for a third party, is one and the same thing.[13]

Alienation can be overcome only in the last instance, which is physicality, matter, or the real of suffering and of "instincts." Emancipation from any form of oppression is emancipation from alienation which stems from abstraction. Abstraction is a philosophical procedure of creating an auto-referential "universe of meaning," which is detached from the real of human existence in order to objectify it, master it, and exploit it. Subjects of abstrac-

---

[13] Karl Marx, "Third Manuscript: Critique of Hegel's Philosophy in General," in Marx, *Economic and Philosophic Manuscripts of 1844*, available at http://www.marxists.org/archive/marx/works/1844/manuscripts/hegel.htm.

tion and alienation are not only the proletariat and the precariat, but also the exploiters in the capitalist era. Emancipation is possible only if we all are equally called to "give up our abstractions" (Marx). All of us are, in the last instance, radically vulnerable pre-subjective identities that revolt against exploitation and violence. This messianic revolt and resistance should be directed against the subject positions which maintain alienation and use the abstraction to exploit, subjugate, and alienate its species.

The brutality of exploiting what Laruelle terms "the human-in-human" (the pre-subjective instance of the real, or the instance of the lived that the human in the last instance is), the infliction of pain on others, or profit from exploitative violence, is enabled only if the human being is objectified as labor and nature is objectified as a means of production and subsistence. Nature certainly provides subsistence, but alienation from and within it occurs when it is objectified. Alienation's immediate result is violence, subjugation, and exploitation (of all and everyone subject to alienation).

> Thus, if the product of his labor, his labor objectified, is for him an alien, hostile, powerful object independent of him, then his position towards it is such that someone else is master of this object, someone who is alien, hostile, powerful, and independent of him. If he treats his own activity as an unfree activity, then he treats it as an activity performed in the service, under the dominion, the coercion, and the yoke of another man.[14]

Estrangement of labor, estrangement from within the species and other species, and also estrangement from oneself—appearing as objectifying oneself as labor force or as "abstract activity and a belly"—can be overcome by the radical procedure of immanently correlating with the site of the real of suffering and joy, which in the last instance is not an abstraction (i.e., the bodily or the "sensuousness" of the self).[15] Recuperating the determination-in-the-last-instance of the human as the physical, material, bodily, or rooted in and ultimately determined by "nature," aims at the realization of the human animal as a non-human or non-animal. In other words, the human species can transcend alienation—hence, oppression—only by radically grounding itself in its material or real humanity, one that precedes philosophy, and

---

[14] Marx, "First Manuscript: Estranged Labor," in Marx, *Economic and Philosophic Manuscripts of 1844.*
[15] Karl Marx, "First Manuscript: Wages of Labour," in Marx, *Economic and Philosophical Manuscripts of 1844*, available at http://www.marxists.org/archive/marx/works/1844/manuscripts/wages.htm.

ultimately, language. The human can come to its fullest realization by succumbing to the immanence of human animality (the human without humanism), through following the syntax of the real that it dictates in the processes of cognition and metaphysics it prompts.

IV. Metaphysics in Radical Terms and as Real Necessity

François Laruelle's book, entitled *Théorie des Etrangers: Science des hommes, démocratie et non-psychanalyse* (1995), is a project of non-philosophical procedure which radicalizes Lacanian psychoanalysis to what Laruelle terms as "non-analysis."[16] Namely, it aims to radicalize psychoanalysis by producing conceptual means for it to account for the workings of the instance of the real and its conditioning effects on signifying processes. The real of the human-in-human, according to Laruelle's non-analysis, inevitably mediates itself through the process of estranging oneself from the real that one is. One has to transpose oneself into a lingually conceived self, into a subject, in order to mediate the real (one is) to the others and to oneself. Prior to becoming a subject one becomes a "Stranger," which is "radical subjectivity."[17] Unlike the subject which can emerge only as the result of a fully completed estrangement from the lived (the real), and which is a signifying position or virtually a sheer function (of the self), the Stranger is affected by the immanence of the process of estrangement. It is concrete, made of transcendental material (language), and is in unilateral affirmation of the dyad that is consisted of the real and the transcendental (language). In its gesture of estrangement, the Stranger transcends the real while experiencing the process of estrangment from the real that he or she has (in the last instance) insofar lived. The real from which one alienates oneself is objectified so that one can transcend the real that one is. Thus, one transcends oneself, the self in the last instance, or the self-in-the-real, so one is rendered an object of control and auto-production by the language and through the function of the linguistically competent subject.

The Stranger is still in the real (of estrangement) while the trauma of the primal metaphysical procedure takes place—that of "becoming stranger to oneself" or sensing the core of oneself as an exteriority. Laruelle insists the "concreteness" of the Stranger is not "empirico-metaphysical," but rather "transcendental." My claim is that this gesture is fundamentally metaphysical. Scientific thought is transcendental with respect to the unruly real. It creates

---

[16] François Laruelle, *Théorie des Etrangers: Science des hommes, démocratie et non-psychanalyse* (Paris: Éditions Kimé, 1995).
[17] Laruelle, *Théorie des Étrangers*, 196.

designs and produces abstractions which aim to explain the real. The experience of estrangement, however, is existentially conditioning—or, in philosophical vocabulary, "ontological"—as it introduces the "spectrality" of language or thought as an inalienable element of the self. The paradox, which, non-philosophically speaking is falsehood and does not exist, engenders the creation of religion, philosophy, science, or the "human species" as the most metaphysical animal (Other animals experience metaphysical states as well, as I have been convinced by Giorgio Agamben's treatise "The Open."). Wondering, or θαῦμα, over the necessity of the production of the spectral self and the world of spectrality, wondering if the real self is (in) the real itself, or if the truth of it (what we make out of it as linguistic subjects) is more real (than the real devoid of meaning/truth), prompts metaphysics. When metaphysics conditions the physical to the extent that it perverts its "life-increasing" (Spinoza) impulses, or the conatus of survival urging "life-decreasing" activities (such as alienated labor and fruits of that labor), that means that "a sufficient thought," viz. thought that usurps the status of the real conditions the world. It conditions the world politico-economically as well as philosophically, causing radical subjection and exploitation of the "real" and the "sensuous" (Marx). By objectifying the "material" (without philosophical materialism), absolute abstraction has effaced any trace of the experience of estrangement as immanent, and has committed the perfect crime against the real (Baudrillard) by convincing the world that it (abstraction) has always been the only real that ever existed. According to this logic, the "senseless real" is not real. What makes sense and what is real have been equated.

In non-philosophy, the equation at issue is called "decisionism," which is what defines philosophy. This is, according to Laruelle, the defining trait of any and all philosophy, and is one of the facets of the principle of sufficient philosophy, as discussed in the previous chapter.[18] Namely, it decides a priori what the real is, and according to this grounding definition only, carries out all further investigations of the real and different realities. Scientific approach, both according to Laruelle and Marx, permits that thought is always "surprised" by the real, and that gaps and inconsistencies in a system of thought are allowed, and moreover, are invited and unavoidable since thought succumbs to the "real" rather than to the "real's meaning." Therefore, the transcendental—which is the substance of any form of thought—is also the material that scientific thought is made of. The necessary procedure of estrangement is, however, metaphysical.

The metaphysical is the effect of the necessary procedure of

---

[18] François Laruelle, *Philosophie et non-philosophie* (Liège and Brussels: Mardaga, 1989), 45ff.

estrangement, of the unavoidability to create the spectral doublet of the physical self, and to transcend physicality in the form of re-creating oneself as an idea of oneself. To paraphrase Lacan, the mirror image of the self tends to occupy the position of the real self. It is endowed with the ambition to become "more real than the real." In this sense, it is identical with the tendencies of philosophy. Nonetheless, the primary metaphysical experience takes place in the mist of vagueness of the concept and physicality of the real. The subject constituting process of estrangement is a sensation, as it involves physicality and intense mental experience which precedes pure concept, but nonetheless represents a process of conceptualization. This process is what Laruelle would call an instance of the lived (*vécu*), rather than an exclusively intellectual procedure which follows the laws of logic and discipline of maintaining a consistent "universe of meaning." Although it seeks to establish control over the real, it also seeks to "fill" the spectral self with it in order for the real to legitimize the idea of the self. It seeks not to find itself, but to remain in the fissure of the split between the idea-(of)-self and the real, by ensuring the real will "legitimize" the idea by finding itself at home with or in it.

Philosophy enters the scene when meaning seeks to legitimize the real upon the basis of radical detachment and indifference to it; even the reverse direction of inter-legitimization, in the last instance, consists in the same gesture: by claiming that the real is reflected by thought in its totality, one produces a reality that should act in the stead of the real (as a more perfect real than the real itself). Concurring with Laruelle, let us say that the equation established between thought and the real is the essential procedure of philosophy (i.e., its decisionism). It presupposes overcoming the anxiety that is produced by the real seemingly splitting into two when the idea of the self emerges as a reality in its own right. As for the metaphysical—in the sense that I am using the word here—its struggle with the real and the possibility of detachment of the spectral self from the real is an experience of anxiety, pain, and pleasure. In the last instance it is an experience, a pure instance of the lived (Laruelle) or the real, albeit involving transcendental operations (i.e., the mental processes of duplication of the real).

The processes of alienation that are foundational for the subject create a metaphysical drama that determines grand ideologies, universes of meaning (philosophies, political and economic contracts), and the human species' "being-before-death" and sexuality. Alienation is the operation that is conditional for the possibility of exploitation; it enables the severing from the "state of innocence" in which the naive and radical human is in awe of the real (of) life, so that the possibility of objectifying the real of other living beings or oneself is inconceivable. This procedure of objectification is indispensible; it is enabled by the operation of alienation from oneself, others, the "sensuous life" (Marx), and the real. Only by virtue of absolute alienation, which brings about absolute abstraction, and only by abstraction's usurpation of the position of the real (as "the most perfect real"), has the criminal rule of capitalism been inaugurated and maintained. Such a process is impossible without the immanently philosophical operation of "gradation of the real," according to which the truer a reality is, "the more real" it is. What is specific of capitalism and modernity is the fact, unlike in the premodern times when the "most real reality" was somewhere else, in a different universe ("the world of ideas", the Kingdom of God) the "ever perfecting real" occupies the material space and temporality of the human. Thus, it is a sheer operation; it is a methodological procedure and a ruse. It does not believe in the possibility of a better and more perfect universe, but only in the intellectual trick which constitutes a reality in its own right. It simulates the material reality and also operates with it, but it is concerned with it only in order to spectralize and accomplish its total exploitation. The materialism of contemporary capitalist society is deprived of a sense of realness, since the real is replaced by operations of abstraction which is made of the meanings that we have assigned to the real and materiality. Both capitalist and modern philosophy's materialism is about the unstoppable tendency—since it is an immanent tendency—to transpose "sensuous matter" into the meanings that can be attached and thereof be reduced from it. Perversely, its materialism is without matter. The ruse of abstraction has mathematized matter and body, transforming economy into finances and sensations into psychological phenomena subject to biopolitical control. To speculate with resources, with lives, has brought about the rule of absolute speculation: management of realities and financial speculation as economy.

The political task of greatest urgency today is to emancipate the radically metaphysical and the "sensuous life" (the material without materialism, and the real without philosophical realism) from the rule of abstraction. This is the core of Marx's call for emancipation of the "human species." This call has never been answered through any other means except philosophy. "Dialectical materialism" is philosophically sufficient, put in Laruellian terms. Namely, it is a sufficient principle to determine and decide what is real. Not to betray this principle—not to betray the principles of its doctrine—has become more important than not to betray the real which invites the doctrine to examine its tenets. Abstraction has ruled Marxism, and Marxism has ruled through abstraction, for more than a century. Communist parties and states of the 20th century, in spite of their numerous differences, have had one thing in common—the real, material, and sensuous human life was the objectifiable material and means that served their greater political goal. Marx explains, saying, "The perfect political state is, by its nature, man's species-life, as opposed to his material life."[19]

If "giving up one's abstractions" (Marx) is the central and most important task of the science that Marx invents and attempts to institute, then the task is to emancipate the necessary and primitive metaphysics mediating the immediate real. Economic emancipation and other important forms of social emancipation would only follow consequentially. The first task is to overcome the underlying alienation enabling the dichotomy between state politics and the civil society, between the "spiritual" or religion and the secular, and finally, to overcome phantomal existence and its suffocation of "real life":

> The perfect political state is, by its nature, man's species-life, as opposed to his material life. All the preconditions of this egoistic life continue to exist in civil society outside the sphere of the state, but as qualities of civil society. Where the political state has attained its true development, man—not only in thought, in consciousness, but in reality, in life—leads a twofold life, a heavenly and an earthly life: life in the political community, in which he considers himself a communal being, and life in civil society, in which he acts as a private individual, regards other men as a means, degrades himself into a means, and becomes the plaything of alien powers. The relation of the political state to civil society is just as spiritual as the relations of heaven to earth. The political state stands in the same opposition to civil society, and it prevails over the latter in the same way as religion prevails over the narrowness of the secular world—i.e., by likewise having always to acknowledge it, to restore it, and allow itself to be dominated by it. In his most immediate reality, in civil society, man is a secular being. Here, where he regards himself as a real individual, and is so regarded by others, he is a fictitious phenomenon. In the state, on the other hand, where man is regarded as a species-being, he is the imaginary member of an illusory sovereignty, is deprived of his real individual life and endowed with an unreal universality.[20]

Instead of simply concluding with this quote by Marx, let us remind ourselves that so far, both the bourgeois and communist regimes have managed to maintain and deepen these divisions. They

---

[19] Karl Marx, "On the Jewish Question," *Deutsch-Französische Jahrbücher*, February 1844, available at http://www.marxists.org/archive/marx/works/1844/jewish-question/.
[20] Marx, "On the Jewish Question."

have accomplished this through the absolute rule of abstraction and the brutal subjugation of materiality.

3: Metaphysics of the Finance Economy

Radicalization as the Method of Revoking Real Economy

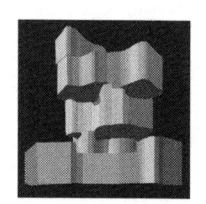

If "giving up our abstractions" is the central and most important task of the science that Marx invents and attempts to institute, then I would argue that the following task should be to emancipate the metaphysics, or the object of that science, from the authority of philosophy. It is the primitive and radical metaphysics of the inevitable gesture of mediating the immediate real that ought to be salvaged through non-philosophical scientific operations with the *chôra* of metaphysical thought. Economic emancipation and other important forms of social emancipation would only follow consequentially. I would sum up Marx's project as follows: the central task is to overcome the underlying philosophical alienation that enables the dichotomies of state politics and civil society of the "spiritual" (or religious) and the secular (of "use value" and "surplus value"). Finally, the task of Marxist science is to serve a political struggle that seeks to overcome the phantomal existence that is shaped by wage labor and surplus value. The universe, ruled by surplus value, is guided by the impulse to suffocate real life and its material grounding, which is represented as use value.

To radicalize metaphysics is to render it transcendental in the last instance, to acknowledge it as the necessary mediator or core of radical subjectivity, which Laruelle terms "the Stranger." The subject establishes a relation of exteriority to it, and seen in its last instance (or radically and inalienably),[1] it is the Stranger at the

---

[1] François Laruelle, *Théorie des Etrangers: Science des hommes, démocratie*

heart of the human-in-human. This concept admits and affirms the dyad between the real and the lived, or "le joui sans jouissance" of the human in the last instance and the subject, while remaining radically descriptive or minimally transcendental.[2] This affirmation of the dyad engenders the radical subjectivity or the "figure of the Stranger." The sense of pain of the original estrangement, the sense of appropriation of this pain that transmutes the painful lived into joy, and the sense of possession, being at home, or of inalienable belonging with the Stranger emerging from the heart of our mute self, is the most immediate form of radical metaphysics.

My claim is that there is no exit from metaphysics. We are metaphysical creatures inasmuch as we are material ones, with the latter always already inviting the former. However, an exit from the disciplining and hallucinatory grasp of philosophical metaphysics is possible, as both Marx and Laruelle have shown. The effect of such exit is not only intellectual or academic, but also social. Philosophical decisionism, in absolute form, is the essence of politics and the capitalist economy, which I will try to demonstrate further in this chapter. Nonetheless, the ideas of political systems and the possibilities of thinkable political horizons remains or becomes ever more detached from the economic logic of the liberal, pseudo-materialistic, and individualist philosophy of exploitation through capitalist alienation.

Philosophical entrapment of metaphysics is constituted by the so-called amphibology of "the being" and the real, and of the "essence" and "the being."[3] I would like to propose a non-philosophical procedure of radicalizing metaphysics through unilateralizing the dyad, by situating it in the "material self" as its subject. Through the necessary and radical estrangement, or in Laruelle's terms, through the emergence of the figure of the Stranger at the core of the real or the human-in-human, the inception of the metaphysical is constitutive of every subjectivization. This inception is painful, but nonetheless inevitable and always already in place without being the product of a philosophical intention. Radicalizing metaphysics would result in furnishing the grounds for a realist, or non-philosophically materialist, theory of the human universe. The radical dyad is at the heart of the material self that has trouble claiming its own self as its own. Affirming this dyad means affirming the real of the trauma that it produces. It also means affirming its reality instead of erasing it through a second gesture, which is always philosophical (which includes religion, and in particular, Abrahamic theologies).

---

et non-psychanalyse (Paris: Éditions Kimé, 1995), 196 : "'Radical' ne signifie pas autre chose qu'inaliénable ou que de-dernière-instance."

[2] Larulle, *Théorie des Etrangers*, 221–223.

[3] A Laruellian term, explained in the previous chapters.

I. The Source of the Capitalist Drive: Dispossession Rather than Possession

The sense of alienation begins at the level of subject's constitution; it is this sense of dispossession that begets the grounding anxiety that creates philosophy as a panic and totalitarian response. Capitalist hyper-production of "added value" (added to the surplus value) represents a total colonization of society and material life by philosophy as the totalitarian response to a metaphysical need. This metaphysical need is materially grounded. The hysteria of private possession and of possessing the truth (of the real) as if it were the real itself aims to compensate for this primordial sense of dispossession. Can the problem of primordial dispossession be solved through the gesture of erasing it, and if done so, wouldn't that be a properly philosophical response? So, is the abolition of the desire for any form of possession or property the true goal of communism, seen as the result of the non-philosophical science that Marx attempts to establish? If alienation created through wage labor represents exacerbation of the sense of grounding dispossession, then capitalism is certainly not the solution to it, in spite of its ceaseless compulsion to be precisely that (for the chosen few and on the expense of the rest of the objectified humanity). Therefore, a sense of possession is not what defines capital and the capitalist self; it is rather the insatiable urge for it that originates in the grounding dispossession. The capitalist drive creates an unstoppable process of alienation of labor, objectifying human labor and the suffering behind it. Numeric or speculative values of pleasure or sources of pleasure (measured in money) derives from the urge toward ever-greater perfection through an abstraction of the needs that are only in their last instance material. In short, the founding operation of capitalist society is the dispossession of the material from its own metaphysical transposition (for example, of the worker from her metaphysics of work, or of the lover from his metaphysics of pleasure). The cancelling of radical or primitive metaphysics is the defining prerequisite of philosophical and capitalist metaphysics.

At the beginning of the 21st century, the economy is no longer an economy in the proper sense of the word. Instead, it is an instrument of finances that postures as an economy in its own right. The "Finance industry" establishes amphibology with the real economy, which is linked to material production of material consumables (a term explained below). The purely symbolic and linguistic (insofar as a matter of signification) value of money is no longer added to the material or use value. It is utterly detached from it. It has become auto-referential, and its value is measured only according to hypothetical measurements in hypothetical systems of measuring. According to *The Financial Crisis Inquiry Report* published by the US Government in 2011,[4] the great financial crisis that began in 2008 (and in 2014, it seems, it is here to stay), or the "recession," was the result of "wrong estimations of the ranking agencies and the banks" about the worth of "derivatives," "securities," and other forms of derivation of financial value from other financial values with no direct reference to any real or physical property or use value (indirectly and in the last instance, after a virtually endless line of mediations, there is always reference to an estimation of the worth of a material property). The authors of the report write:

> In the years leading up to the crisis, too many financial institutions, as well as too many households, borrowed to the hilt, leaving them vulnerable to financial distress or ruin if the value of their investments declined even modestly. For example, as of 2007, the five major investment banks—Bear Stearns, Goldman Sachs, Lehman Brothers, Merrill Lynch, and Morgan Stanley—were operating with extraordinarily thin capital. By one measure, their leverage ratios were as high as 40 to 1, meaning for every $40 in assets, there was only 1$ in capital to cover losses. Less than a 3$ drop in asset values could wipe out a firm. To make matters worse, much of their borrowing was short-term, in the overnight market—meaning the borrowing had to be renewed each and every day. For example, at the end of 2007, Bear Stearns had $11.8 billion in equity and $383.6 billion in liabilities and was borrowing as much as $70 billion in the overnight market. It was the equivalent of a small business with $50.000 in equity borrowing $1.6 million, with $296,750 of that due each and every day. One can't really ask, "What were they thinking?" when it seems that too many of them were thinking alike. And the leverage was often hidden—in derivatives positions, in off-balance-sheet entities, and through "window dressing" of financial reports available to the investing public.[5]

Evidently, what was traded was not the material value (or the use value) of a material or physical object together with its estimated surplus value. The surplus value only entered into

---

[4] Financial Crisis Inquiry Commission [FCIC], *The Financial Crisis Inquiry Report: Final Report of the National Commission on the Causes of the Financial and Economic Crisis in the United States* (Washington, DC: U.S. Government Publishing Office, 2011), xix–xx; available at http://www.gpo.gov/fdsys/pkg/GPO-FCIC/content-detail.html.
[5] FCIC, *The Financial Crisis Inquiry Report*, xx.

exchange after it had become completely detached from any reference to or relevance with use value. Negligence and squander of the real value of mortgages, or the fact that their real financial value had been unchecked or falsified, was not the main reason for "the collapse of the financial system" in 2008. The possibility of an utterly speculative trade, one that is based on pure abstractions of values and the complete detachment from the material (reflected in use value), is the generator of the problem. Moreover, this represents the very foundation of investment banking and the "investment business" as a form of economy. As we can see in the report quoted above, the "investment economy" is not based on capital in the classical sense of the word. It is not even based on capital in the financial sense, which implies its translatability into the material. Its foundations lie in the "thin air" of its capacities to rank, estimate, evaluate, predict, create, and control processes in the financial market.

There is nothing material in the 21st century's form of capitalism. Contemporary capitalism is not only based on "immaterial labor," as Negri and Hardt claim,[6] but also on pure abstraction and elevation to the immateriality of both labor and capital. This situation is the result of the complete mathematization and speculation of the real. The 662 pages of T*he Financial Crisis Inquiry Report* by the US Government (quoted above) displays the blatant truth that the concept (and all of its possible realities) of "investment banking" itself is indiscernible from the so called "shadow banking system." In the last instance it is speculative, and while speculating it interprets the material according to its own immanent rules (of speculation) and is in no way bound by the "primitive real." The real that has not been transformed into a meaning, signification, or value is the "primitive," unruly real that seems to be non-existent unless given shape and value by the speculative mind. Investment banking, in the last instance, is determined by the practice of conducting "expertise" and speculation about the immaterial value (surplus or financial value) behind—or derived from—material worth:

> First, we describe the phenomenal growth of the shadow banking system—the investment banks, most prominently, but also other financial institutions—that freely operated in capital markets beyond the reach of the regulatory apparatus that had been put in place in the wake of the crash of 1929 and the Great Depression. This new system threatened the once-dominant traditional commercial banks, and they took their grievances to their regulators

[6] Michael Hardt and Antonio Negri, *Multitudes: War and Democracy in the Age of Empire* (New York: Penguin, 2004).

and to Congress, which slowly but steadily removed long-standing restrictions and helped banks break out of their traditional mold and join the feverish growth. As a result, two parallel financial system of enormous scale emerged.[7]

Capitalism is grounded in fetishization, wrote Marx. The contemporary economy is, in the last instance, determined by fetishism. Marx's fetishization may have been borrowed from the studies of religion that he was familiar with when he was writing the first volume of *Capital*, but its meaning is very precise in terms of understanding the split between and surplus value, and also how the latter engenders the very logic of money as capital:

> M-M'. We have here the original starting-point of capital, money in the formula M-C -M' reduced to its two extremes M—M', in which M'=M+DM, money creating more money. It is the primary and general formula of capital reduced to a meaningless condensation. It is ready capital, a unity of the process of production and the process of circulation, and hence capital yielding a definite surplus-value in a particular period of time. In the form of interest-bearing capital this appears directly, unassisted by the processes of production and circulation. Capital appears as a mysterious and self-creating source of interest—the source of its own increase. The thing (money, commodity, value) is now capital even as a mere thing, and capital appears as a mere thing. [...] The social relation is consummated in the relation of a thing, of money, to itself. Instead of the actual transformation of money into capital, we see here only form without content. As in the case of labour-power, the use-value of money here is its capacity of creating value—a value greater than it contains. Money as money is potentially self-expanding value and is loaned out as such—which is the form of sale for this singular commodity.[8]

If capitalism is determined in the last instance by what Marx calls "fetishism," and if the latter is determined as speculative (hence, philosophical),[9] it is bound to end up (and also end) as

---

[7] FCIC, *The Financial Crisis Inquiry Report*, 27–28.
[8] Karl Marx, "Externalization of the Relations of Capital in the Form of Interest-Bearing Capital," in Karl Marx, *Capital: A Critique of Political Economy*, Vol. 3 (Moscow: Progress Publishers, 1959), available at https://www.marxists.org/archive/marx/works/1867-c1/.
[9] As explained in the previous chapters, Marx equates philosophy with the abstract or the metaphysical (even when it is defined as «materialistic»), and it is difficult to determine if he sees any intrinsic possibility for it to

a "financial economy" instead of a "real economy." By instituting the "fiat money" principle at its very origins, the possibility of an economy unattached to any material or use value (or in some economic vocabularies "objective value") has been introduced. Moreover, speculation, and therefore detachment from the real, is the determination in the last instance and the vector of a capitalist economy.

II. Pure Speculation as the Determination in the Last Instance of Capitalism as Philosophy

The detachment from use value produces and sustains the defining relevance of the pretension that the speculative logic of the economy determines or engineers the use value itself. The implication is, therefore, that direct and material needs can be subsumed under fetish based needs. This desire is disciplined by the capitalist jouissance; it operates upon the physical that attempts to mould it. As language governs the body and as philosophy governs the real, these "speculative needs" are more urgent than material ones. *A philosophy as the world or the world as philosophy, specifically defined by capitalism, is what sustains these processes and maintains capital's circulation of significance.*

The philosophical/capitalist mirror of desires and needs falls asunder when confronted by the material urgency of suffering bodies. The pain, hunger, and rage created by the urgency of survival dispels the speculum of detached needs, which are inscribed in the universe of "what matters in human life." When economic resources that provide for material (and "spiritual" as used in Marx's texts) needs and interests are exhausted and survival is under threat, the speculum of capitalism and philosophy becomes "the bubble" that *The Financial Crisis Inquiry Report* talks about.

In 2008, the bubble burst and thereupon the state intervened. This intervention could not, however, be speculative. It had to draw on the material resources of its citizens: mortgages defaulted in the US and austerity cuts introduced in the EU. This brute material had to enter the scene of finances. The material, in the guise of defaulted mortgages and destroyed livelihoods, provided the grounds for the resurrection of a universe of nothing but signification—of finances and the speculative "finance industry." The world made of the "estimation" of material had to be saved by a holocaust of the material. In the end, it wasn't the monetary value added to the material use value and labor force, but the sheer bricks of land, life (as labor force), and livelihood of the labor force that had to ensure the survival of the banks and the resurrection of

detach itself from the metaphysical determination in the last instance.

the specter (namely, the market of speculation). These bricks and livelihoods were destroyed as soon as they were translated into "derivatives."

The 2008 crisis was the first instance in the history of capitalism when the speculative foundation was proven untenable unless supported by matter and, in the last instance, determined by the real and/or the physical. Contemporary economics is the product of philosophical determination in the last instance, which postulates that the brute material is meaningless unless signified as monetary value. All ought to become pure signification since the material in itself is meaningless and worthless in the human universe which is made of signs, exchanges of signification, and communication. My generalization is that, according to the ruling visions of authority today, the essence of economy, or the logic of the market, has its own intrinsic laws unattached to the basic survival needs of human and non-human animals. In the last instance, contemporary economics is determined by the transcendental. Namely, it is determined by a philosophical decision on what reality is, this decision institutes itself as more real than the real itself. The transcendental postulation that constitutes this determination in the last instance is Kantian and post-Kantian. In other words, it is always already postmodern. The capitalist vision of the world is essentially philosophical.

It is a vision determined by its decisionism, rather than by the authority of the real without the "added value" of philosophical or economical meaning. With this explanation of capitalism in view, I concur with the accelerationist manifesto of Nick Srnicek and Alex Wiliams, inspired by Nick Land's theory of accelerationism, according to which speeding up capitalism's functioning according to its inherent logic could be revolutionary.[10] Nonetheless, acceleration itself is immanent to a capitalist political economy. The sheer introduction of the gesture of acceleration to what already accelerates itself unstoppably does not constitute an intervention (let alone a revolution). Emancipation of the processes of acceleration from the bourgeois grip and its subsequent radical socialization (transformation into commons rather than the private property of a few individuals) is required in order to transcend capitalism and begin the creation of a socialist society.

This increasingly accelerated capitalism will inevitably take its political-economic infrastructure and specter of "finance industry" to the stage of hitting against the bedrock of the real, and as a result, to the falling asunder of its auto-referential

---

[10] Nick Srnicek and Alex Williams, "#Accelerate: Manifesto for an Accelerationist Politics, Critical Legal Thinking" (weblog), May 14, 2013, http://criticallegalthinking.com/2013/05/14/accelerate-manifesto-for-an-accelerationist-politics.

meaninglessness. The real is not speculative; it is "the physical and sensuous" (Marx). It is the real-of-the-human that is presubjective and prelingual.[11] Therefore, the revolts in city squares, the sit-ins, the occupation of space, and as Benjamin Noys argues, the overall slowing down and resistance to the temporal strategies of capital is one of the effective forms of resistance.[12] In a parallel fashion, another form of resistance is to accelerate the speed of speculative finance in order for it to hit against the impossibility of the real that consists of the lack of material resources. If the finance industry capitalizes on the ruse of projections about the worth of the material (all assets backed by material property), the absence of anything to estimate and project about will end.[13] The surplus value and use value will inevitably dissociate when there are disproportionately more empty buildings than populated ones, by way of an inflation of defaulted mortgages and devaluated assets. Evidently, an apocalyptic landscape is necessary for a new political horizon to appear. Nick Land's accelerationist nihilism also could be understood in this sense—this is where I identify its revolutionary potential (regardless of whether Land positions himself right or left).[14]

The financial crisis in 2008 proved wrong the philosophical grounding of the modern economy as essentially materialistic and conveyed its purely transcendental and speculative foundations. The sobering effect of the real materialized in the form of trauma caused by defaulted mortgages, lost homes, and lost jobs dispelled the mathematical purity of contemporary economy as financial in its last instance. In spite of the blow of the real that burst the global financial bubble in 2008, six years later, the fetish or specter of money rules stronger than ever. Austerity cuts aim at saving speculation itself. Remorseless saving has been imposed not only on social strata, but also on entire countries. The most prominent case in Europe is that of Greece. Greece's real economy is practically dead because of fictitious debt—being "interest rates" and speculation on the worth of estimation (money). *The real economy is dying in the name of the industry that produces signification and value.* The finance industry is now alive and well, in perfect detachment from the material or use worth, whereas its material resources are progressively impoverished and

---

[11] François Laruelle, *Ethique de l'Étranger* (Paris: Éditions Kimé, 2000), 259.
[12] Benjamin Noys, "The War of Time: Occupation, Resistance, Communization, *Identities: Journal for Politics, Gender and Culture* 10.1-2 (2013): 83–92.
[13] Brett Scott, *The Heretic Guide to Global Finance: Hacking the Future of Money* (London: Pluto Press, 2013).
[14] Nick Land, *Fanged Noumena: Collected Writings 1987-2007*, eds. Ray Brassier and Robin McKay (Falmouth, UK: Urbanomic, 2011).

marked for destruction. The vampirism of the finance industry and its political elites is sucking out the life of all that is living on this planet. The exploitation and destruction of nature—which includes the human race—leaves us with a spectral universe that will soon be inhabitable for its vampires too. Currently, the real is suppressed by the (essentially capitalist) universe of speculation, both in the philosophical sense and in the sense of the speculative mind of gaming.

> Herb Sandler, the co-founder of the mortgage lender Golden West Financial corporation, which was heavily loaded with option ARM loans, wrote a letter to officials at the Federal Reserve, the FDIC, the OTS, and the OCC warning that regulators were "too dependent" on ratings agencies and "there is a high potential for gaming when virtually any asset can be churned through securitization and transformed into a AAA-rated asset, and when a multi-billion dollar industry is all too eager to facilitate this alchemy.[15]

III. The Economy is Always Already Political

Gaming includes risk, but the type of gaming which grounds the so-called finance industry does not presuppose risk in the last instance, i.e. by material defaulting and materially or physically experienced loss. In the last instance, when the gamers collided with the rock of the real—the material threat to "their way of life"—they asked for a government bailout and they got it. Apparently, there is direct relationship between the banking industry and the government, at least in the US and in the European Union, as has been proven since the 2008 financial crash. Intervention of the state in the affairs of economy that creates use value (apart from or in addition to the surplus value) is understandable. However, the motivation of the state to intervene in the so-called finance industry in order to save it and maintain economic stability is utterly vague. How does the stability of investment banks and their funds serve general economic stability, one linked to material production, consumption, and sustainability?

Investment banking concerns turning investments into investments, betting on the viability of investments, and selling those speculations to other investment speculators. It serves all sorts of funds whose activity comes down to the trade of its assessment, of the best guess or speculation about of the financial worth of something which has only indirect or meditated—if any—material worth. The material determination in the last

[15] FCIC, *The Financial Crisis Inquiry Report*, 48.

instance is not the subject of trade in investment banking, and is hardly its determination in the last instance.

In the last instance, the investment (and/or banking) industry has no effect on the real industry (at least not a productive one). So why is the maintained stability of the finance market so important for the economic stability of a country? How come it is more important than the "material industry" or the so-called real economy? This question departs from the fact that the bailout of the former takes place at the detriment of the latter.

> This resilience led many executives and regulators to presume the financial system hadachieved unprecedented stability and strong risk management. The Wall Street banks' pivotal role in the Enron debacle did not seem to trouble senior Fed officials. In a memorandum to the FCIC, Richard Spillenkothen described a presentation to the Board of Governors in which some Fed governors received details of the banks' complicity "coolly" and were "clearly unimpressed" by analysts' findings. "The message to some supervisory staff was neither ambiguous nor subtle," Spillenkothen wrote. Earlier in the decade, he remembered, senior economists at the Fed had called Enron an example of a derivatives market participant successfully regulated by marketdiscipline without government oversight.[16]

Regardless of the eventual presence/absence of oversight, government intervention was required and considered legitimate since it is the government's responsibility to preserve the economic stability of a country (and through that of all other forms of social stability). This means that the use value necessary for life, both for the physical and "spiritual" (as in Marx's texts, i.e., as attached and directly issuing from the physical) survival of the ordinary citizens, had to be transformed into surplus value that serves the stability of the financial market. In other words, the material is annulled by its transformation into the purely speculative. Thus, the use value is barred by its total transformation into surplus value and the sole purpose of this process is to sustain a universe of pure surplus value.

How important is the health of the investment and banking industry, or the health and stability of hedge funds and insurance companies, for the survival of the so-called real economy? How has the crisis of the investment industry really affected the material production of tangible use value? If the banking industry can be viewed as an industry in its own right that can remain

---

[16] FCIC, *The Financial Crisis Inquiry Report*, 60.

fundamentally detached from the real economy, how important is it for a country's stability to insure the survival and preservation of this autonomous universe? The 2008 financial crisis has certainly affected all those who have had to default on their house loans or who have lost social benefits. If that is the case, then the US Government's bailout of big investors brought more danger than stability, and thus: a) a growth of poverty, b) a huge hole in the national budget, and c) preservation of an "industry," which not only does not necessarily support the real economy, but quite to the contrary, immanently contains the tendency to destroy it (the real economy) if that brings more profit.

Hartmann-Wendels et al. (2010, p. 16) define investment banking as the set of "all functions of a bank, which support trading at financial markets." The common opinion in the literature is that investment banking comprises all services which serve financial allocation opportunities, as long as they are provided via securities transactions. Broadly speaking, investment banks assist "the capital market in its function of capital intermediation" (Subramanyam, 2008, p.81). The emergence of financial interm-ediaries is owed to the market imperfections inherent in financial markets.[17]

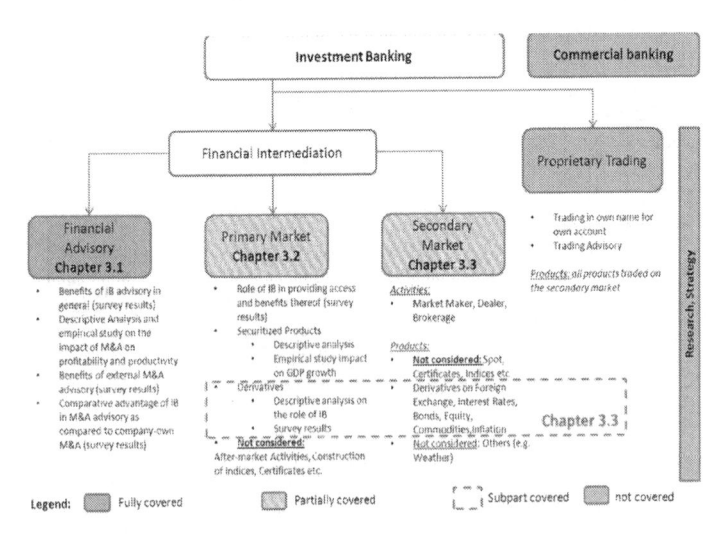

---

[17] Michael Schroeder et al., *The Role of Investment Banking for the German Economy: Final Report for Deutsche Bank* AG, Frankfurt/Main (Mannheim: Zentrum für Europäische Wirtschaftsforschung, 2011), 12. Chart represented above also from Schroeder et al., same page.

This is one attempt at explaining the phenomenon of the "financialization of the economy." Let us examine what other possible definitions there are.

IV. The Change of Marx's Equation

Investment banks do not serve the final beneficiaries of any real economy (i.e., humanity and other living beings). Since the dawn of capitalism, and until the emergence of the "finance economy," industry has been producing material goods. Its goal has always been surplus value, and its vector has always been M→M1, by definition grounded in the production of commodity as the hybrid of use value and surplus value. Use value has been the indispensible intermediary in the creation of surplus value. That is the logic behind the equation M-C-M (money-commodity-money).

At the turn of the 21st century, investment banking assumed the status of the unavoidable intermediary for the investors' main activity (making profit). With the usurpation of the status of the main intermediary in investing, the banking industry has suppressed and finally eliminated the production of use value as the central intermediary for achieving the defining capitalist goal (represented by the M-C-M equation). Since the investment and finance industry have assumed the status of an industry in their own right, and their speculative activity has been assigned the quality of products exchanged on the market, Marx's M-C-M has turned into M-M-M. Commodities produced by the apparently self-sufficient banking industry are purely financial phenomena because they originate in the register of speculation that produces pure signification (money). Commodities produced by the banking industry bear the names of: securities, derivatives, certificates, bonds, equities, etc. The M-M-M cycle is detached from the material and from the primary, secondary, and tertiary economy that continues to satisfy the material needs of human and non-human animals. The chasm that has appeared between the universe of sheer speculation (M-M-M) and that of the physical world and its immediate needs (to which M-C-M was still somehow related) will grow. Finally, the founding of the image and of the tenuous reality of the economic whole the two are presumed to constitute will become inevitable.

When the 2008 financial crisis was declared, the US government decided that the financial institutions facing bankruptcy were "too big to fail" because that would have destabilized the entire economy and they were "too interconnected with other financial institutions."[18] Would such eventual failure have affected the real

[18] FCIC, *The Financial Crisis Inquiry Report*, 386.

economy, in all of its three sectors? Considering that investment banks are detached from commercial banks and work practically with no capital, as the *US Financial Crisis Inquiry Report* informs the reader (quotes are provided above), exactly how would the eventual failure of the banking industry have affected the production of the real economy?

In a collective forum entitled "The Impact of the Financial Crisis on the Real Economy," two authors state that, "the cost of the financial crisis to the real economy has so far remained underexamined, probably because of the difficulty in making such an assessment."[19] This study, which is a policy analysis of the financial crisis's effects on the European, and more particularly, the German economy, makes apparent the fact that the impact of the financial market on the "real market economy" remains a "rather vague phenomenon." It is not only vague to the authors of the study but also to the other academic and non-academic authorities in the area who are cited in it.

> [...] "Finanzdienstleistungsinstitute" is the German equivalent of investment banks. According to the legal definition of the functions of financial service providers ("Finanzdienstleistungsinstitute," §1a KWG), however, the term is rather broad as it also includes other financial service providers besides investment banks. Another issue is raised by the assignment of some financing activities closely intertwined with investment banking activities (e.g. financing of M&A transactions). Although in practice such financing activities may be considered a part of investment banking, the widespread definition of investment banking in academic literature refrains from assigning any financing functions to the term investment banking. Hartmann-Wendels et al. (2010, p. 16) define investment banking as the set of "all functions of a bank, which support trading at financial markets."[20]

In his book from 2013, *Profiting Without Producing*, Costas Lapavitsas claims the same while explaining that the notion of the "financialization of economy" had never even entered the vocabulary or conceptual apparatus of mainstream economics. Nonetheless, this phenomenon has been determining our

---

[19] Daniel Gros and Cinzia Alcidi, "The Crisis and the Real Economy," in *Forum: The Impact of the Financial Crisis on the Real Economy, Intereconomics: Review of European Economic Policy* 45 (2010) [DOI: 10.1007/s10272-010-0320-0]: 4–10..
[20] Gros and Alcidi, "The Crisis and the Real Economy," 12.

economic reality since 2008.[21] Lapavitsas's book also demonstrates how the neoliberal economy is essentially enabled by "monopoly state control over the final means of payment."

The fact that the role of the "finance economy" was completely unexamined when the crisis was declared did not prevent the US government from reacting with bank bailouts, just as it did not prevent EU governments from reacting with budget cuts and other forms of state intervention that aimed to preserve "economic stability." What in fact being saved was the self-enveloped world of the financial market, a self-sufficient universe parasitizing off the rest of society and the economy rather than providing grounds for their survival and growth. On the other hand, the negative affects on the real economy, caused by the reduced spending capacity of the population, were something that could be predicted by every economist, politician, and ordinary citizen. Therefore, what is known to be detrimental to economic stability and growth (material not financial or speculative) was sacrificed in the name of what is known to be utterly unexamined in respect to its affects on the real economy. The states which went on to save their national and the global "financial industries" determined that the intermediary between money making and more money making was more important for overall economic stability than the real economy.

The Enigma of Capital[22] by David Harvey offers a genealogy of the "financialization of economy" and of the financial crisis which occurred after 2008. According to the evidence presented by Harvey, deregulation of finance was the cornerstone of the "new and global financial architecture," which originated in the late 1970s and "was accelerated in 1986 and became unstoppable in the 1990s."[23] Harvey explains that deregulation was a political invention. It was an intervention of the neoliberal governments into the banking system, which aimed to bridge "the gap between what labor was earning and what it could spend."[24] It is interesting to note that the banks were reluctant to embrace absolute liberalism, and hence, absence of any regulation. Therefore, Harvey tells us that "political pressure" had to be used in order to force financial institutions such as Fannie Mae and Freddie Mac to "loosen the credit strings for everyone."[25]

Costas Lapavitsas debunks the myth about the helpless states

[21] Costas Lapavitsas, *Profiting Without Producing: How Finance Exploits Us All* (London: Verso, 2013).
[22] David Harvey, *The Enigma of Capital and the Crisis of Capitalism* (Oxford: Oxford University Press, 2010).
[23] Harvey, *The Enigma of Capital*, 16.
[24] Harvey, *The Enigma of Capital*, 17.
[25] Harvey, *The Enigma of Capital*, 17.

who are incapable of establishing control over the "out of joint capitalism" and imagined "elemental forces" of the naturalized economy. Behind this mirage of unrestrained liberalism lies the truth of the economic and social policies of nation-states. The idea of the absolute liberty of the market, or the imaginary of the natural forces of capital, is made possible by a grounding metaphysical premise about the "naturalness" of a capitalist free market economy. Lapavitsas reminds us that economy has always been political, just as Marx insisted:

> Second, crucial to the ascendancy of private credit money has been its legal convertability into state-backed money created by central banks. The latter is a hybrid form of money: it is partly credit since it is created through credit mechanisms (mostly lending by the central bank to private banks); it is partly fiat since it is inconvertible legal tender that normally rests on the state's promises to pay. This hybrid form of money is the ultimate lever of state power in the realm of finance because it allows the state to provide liquidity and to make payments at critical junctures. Financialization has been stamped by the conscious management of state-backed central bank money through various mechanisms of the state. Central banks have emerged as a leading public institution, typically under a façade of independence. The command exercised by states over central bank money has made sustained intervention in the field of finance possible throughout the period of financialization. The importance of control over state-backed credit money was made clear in the course of the global crisis of the 2000s.[26]

Political pressure that needed to be used in order to install the "system of neoliberalism" proves that absolute liberty of the economy and finance industry is not a natural, self-generated reality. Rather, it is the product of a political decision. Therefore, it is also the product of philosophical decision. It relies on a postulation of reality that is essentially philosophical. This means that one not only postulates cognitively about the real, but also performs a practical gesture of philosophical intervention where thought determines what the real/reality is. While determining the real, the same gesture performs a second subterfuge gesture, and truth substitutes reality. To explain this "decisionism," let us reiterate Laruelle's thesis, which is that what determines any and all philosophy in the last instance thereby produces an amphibology between thought and the real. The most important

[26] Lapavitsas, *Profiting Without Producing*, 70.

product of this amphibology is "the Being."[27] By that same logic, absolute freedom and its supposed innate self-regulation are creations of a philosophical decision which surreptitiously and "amphibologically" instilled in itself as the real, rather than what it really is—a political (and philosophical) decree.

Through the bailouts of investment banks and budget cuts, state authorities have strived to preserve a self-sufficient universe of abstraction called the "finance industry." This universe of pure abstraction seems to be based on the original presupposition that it can survive completely detached from the real or the material world (= the world of defaulted houses and massively reduced reproduction of material goods). Is it possible that this is a philosophical flaw, the result of a mere superstitious misconception? Is it possible that the origin of the crisis consists in a philosophical fallacy, according to which the fetish (money) represents not just a reality but also a worth in its own right rather than mere mediation between two or more material realities? George Soros has accused the German Chancellor Angela Merkel for precisely this—a philosophical fallacy in the ways in which she has dealt with the crisis (i.e., for "misconceptions and taboos" which lead to austerity measures against debtor Eurozone countries such as Greece).[28] In a number of interviews and articles, George Soros, the person who has been one of the main proponents of the "finance industry," unraveled the spectral nature of that same industry which had made him rich. He termed the belief in its realness a misconception. This point is the undercurrent of a central set of arguments in his article on the topic, which was published in October 2013. Let us consider the following quote:

> I can testify from personal experience that investors would flock to Greece once the debt overhang was removed. But the official sector cannot write down its debt, because that would violate a number of taboos, particularly for the ECB.[29]

Certainly, one can never be sure if Merkel suffers from "misconceptions" about the nature of the financial market and its alleged immanently liberal and self-regulating nature, or whether she has made an informed political decision to stick with the policies of neo-liberalism. The same dilemma stands for Barack

---

[27] François Laruelle, *Philosophie et non-philosophie* (Bruxelles-Liege: Pierre Mardaga, 1989), 42 ff.
[28] George Soros, "Angela Merkel's Pyrrhic Victory," *Project Syndicate*, October 7, 2013, http://www.project-syndicate.org/commentary/george-soroson-angela-merkel-s-pyrrhic-victory.
[29] Soros, "Angela Merkel's Pyrrhic Victory."

Obama and his financial policies and political decisions related to the post 2007 crisis. In spite of Soros's advice to the contrary, in 2008 Obama decided to bailout the investment banks. George Soros, one of the most generous financial supporters of Obama's electoral campaign in 2008, advised Obama to nationalize the banks instead, as reported the *Wall Street Journal Online*.[30] It appears unusual that a finance magnate would opt for nationalization of banks while a politician decides to opt for a financialization of the national economy. Once again, it seems viable to claim—and in this respect, I follow David Harvey's argument presented above— that the financialization of global economy is a political project rather than an economic "natural process":

> Fictitious financial capital took control and nobody wanted to stop it because everyone who mattered seemed to be making lots of money. In the US, political contributions from Wall Street soared. Remember Bill Clinton's famous rhetorical question as he took office? 'You mean to tell me that the success of the economic program and my re-election hinges on the Federal Reserve and a bunch of fucking bond traders?' Clinton was nothing if not a quick learner.[31]

In spite of the conscious decision or philosophical ruse to convince the world that "innate absolute freedom" of finance is a natural state of affairs, rather than a state's trick to postpone decisions regarding real economy (as much as possible or almost indefinitely), we might be dealing with misconceptions too. In other words, an informed political decision to pursue neoliberal policies does not exclude the possibility of uninformed misconceptions about its "realness" in the world of material production and reproduction (social, economic and physical). The idea that one could postpone material reality without material consequences is probably a misconception, a fallacy of the fundamentally speculative mind of contemporary capital perpetuating an old metaphysical hierarchy which accords primacy and supremacy to the mental (or "the idea") over the bodily (or "the material").

In the last instance, the self-sufficient and self-enclosed universe of speculation (financial and beyond financial) feeds on the physical world, which it treats as mere material (not matter) for the (re-)production of abstract values. The role of the abstraction in the capitalist world is to (re)produce imperfect matter into numeric perfection (money) and to elevate it to a

---

[30] Luca Di Leo, "Soros Criticizes Obama's Bailouts," *The Wall Street Journal*, March 1, 2010, http://on.wsj.com/1wXziL2..
[31] Harvey, *The Enigma of Capital*, 17.

level where matter transcends itself by being transformed into "materialistic value" or "pure materialism." In spite of the fact that capitalist abstraction has regularly crashed against the material wall of natural resources and human labor, it still believes in its superiority, and hence, the necessity to exploit the physical in order to produce good in the perfect world of pure value. The capitalist drive is grounded in a flawed metaphysical presupposition, not in the greed for the material. *Capitalism is "idealistic" rather than "materialistic." It does not depart from self-interest; rather, it is moved by the eschatology of an elevated and sublimated matter that is more material than matter itself.* It is a pursuit of surplus value, rather than use value, which culminates in the surplus of "pure value." If the motor of social processes is pure value (pure meaning or pure signification), rather than the "immediate interest" (Marx) of the subjugated, one is still trapped in capitalism as the philosophical-in-the-last-instance. One is trapped in a metaphysical illusion and cognitive flaw. That is why surpassing capitalism will mean surpassing philosophy and philosophical metaphysics (since, as demonstrated above, metaphysics does not necessarily have to be philosophical).

4: The Metaphysics of Capitalism and the Socialist Response

I. Metaphysics of Wage Labor as part of Political Theory and Praxis

In *L'introduction au non-marxisme*, François Laruelle argues that Marxism, alongside with psychoanalysis, is a science of the human that non-philosophy seeks to institute and develop. In order for this to come about one needs to rid the Marxian corpus from its philosophical tenets: philosophical and historical materialism as fully developed and self-enveloped system/s of thought and established universes (possible worlds) that are to be enforced. They provide definite and unquestionable answers to the questions of private property, the role of the communist state, what commons are or ought to be, as well as issues of wage labor and what constitutes the proletariat and its rule. Let us remind ourselves, following Laruelle we define decisionism as essentially philosophical. It entails the procedure of establishing duplicity of the real and the truth of it, where the latter posits the former. Such is the status and the procedure of certain concepts central to the Marxist theory, as interpretation of Marx's original text, as "dialectical materialism," and as a few others mentioned above.

Philosophical thought consistently follows the laws of its doctrine, remaining auto-referential and self-sufficient. For the purposes of dismantling the ossified structures, networks, and other forms of systematization of thought, non-philosophy applies the procedure of the radicalization of the argument arriving to its determination in the last instance. For example, according to Laruelle, one has to dismantle the totality of the Marxian authoritative (i.e., philosophical legacy), in order to arrive at Marx's own text as the conceptual point of departure for Marxism. Marx's text ought to be treated as *chôra* rather than as a foreclosed universe of truth established as such, due to the inner laws of the operations of thought pertaining to the doctrine. To treat it as *chôra* implies a theory that is aligned with praxis as its authority in the last instance, whereas the concepts of the theory are treated as mere "transcendental conceptual material." Aligning with praxis or with "the real," in accordance with the non-philosophical procedure of Laruelle, enables the production of a theory (Laruelle) or science (Marx and Laruelle), which is the result of experientially and empirically established positivity produced around the symptoms of the real. The symptoms manifest themselves as trauma or *tuché* experienced physically (the body and mind included). The non-philosophical procedure of radicalization of a postulate goes as far as establishing its determination in the last instance, which is a concept that is by definition affected by the "immanence of the real."[1] Determination in the last instance (*détermination-en-dernière-instance* or *DDI*) is a form of the transcendental, i.e. an operation of thought, but nonetheless philosophically impoverished and transcendentally minimal insofar as it is the effect of the "syntax of the real." Essentially, it is a description of the effect, of the impact of the real, of an intervention of an exteriority which is mere effect, and of trauma that disrupts the automatism of signification (how we habitually think and make sense out of the world and inhabit it). It is the effect of disruption, of obliteration of some meanings and of necessitating the creation of new ones, which is described through determination in the last instance. It is a description of the effect of the real conducted in the immanent way (*de la manière immanente*),[2] in a mode of being affected by the real through the instance of the *lived*. The instance of the lived is an immediacy that is only transposed to the level of the transcendental as the result of an act of linguistic mediation.

In Marx's text, by virtue of applying the procedure that renders it transcendental *chôra*, Laruelle identifies the determination in the last instance (*DDI*) of the theory that it seeks to establish - the notion of labor force. Labor force, the exploitation it entails and its form specifically, as explained by Marx, determines in the last instance the development of the entire theory and points to the practice that should ensue from it. Those who subscribe to some of the central tenets of this theory and wish to escape the circularity and auto-referentiality of philosophy, according to Laruelle, should theorize in a way in which thought succumbs to the authority of the real. Such a process is enabled by following the "syntax of the real" which produces a morphology of thought that is constituted

---

[1] François Laruelle, *Introduction au non-marxisme* (Paris: Presses Universitaires de France), 48.
[2] Laruelle, *Introduction au non-marxisme*, 10.

by the markers of instances of determination in the last instance of any transcendental construct in the text (after it has undergone a procedure of philosophical impoverishment). The *chôra* of Marx's texts does not have to be the only source if the real prompts another conceptual apparatus; other theories are also determined in the last instance by a certain effect of the real. One can arrive to their *DDI*, and thus to their transcendentally impoverished conceptualizations, which can enforce a philosophically nonstandard Marxist argument. However, one should not endorse entire theoretical edifices, but rather draw on the theoretical *chôra*.

The conceptualization of the labor force and its status in Marx's texts, according to non-standard Marxism, makes the term "labor force" the determination-in-the-last-instance of Marxism. Being that it is affected by immanence (or by the real and the lived) also makes it the source of "thought-force" (Laruelle), or thought that immediately induces practice.[3] Only philosophical auto-alienation of theory can alienate the radical core from the practice and the lived of labor-force, and from the subjectivities that it determines in the last instance.

If what moves capitalism is the split between use value and the surplus value, whereby the latter assumes an independent life, and if the detached abstraction of surplus value *re-presented* as the symbolism called "money" can dictate the entire economic-political system by way of subjugating real (or physical) needs, then the concept of "labor force" is one of the determinations in the last instance of Marx's thought. Such is the central claim of Laruelle's *Introduction au non-marxisme*. Alienation from one's physical and spiritual needs, as Marx explained, and amphibologically[4] positing oneself as a commodity that has to be sold on the market of wage labor, is the kernel of capitalist exploitation and subjugation. It is also the lever of the political-economic system of capitalism: it provides the supply and the demand of money and the commodities that ought to be sold at the same time. Thereby, the means of the most basic subsistence are also turned into commodities from wage labor in order to survive and be able to sell itself. In the contradiction of wage labor being both a commodity and the agency that (auto-)sells that same commodity, one not only can identify the moving force of the capitalist machine, but also its impossibility and the source of its downfall. The tormented "rented body," constantly increasing in distress from exhaustion, bad health, and ceaseless fear for its survival and the survival of its dependents, will inevitably crash under the pressure of the theology of money and bourgeois values. At the peak of the contradiction, the prole-

---

[3] Laruelle, *Introduction au non-marxisme*, 48.
[4] François Laruelle, *Philosophie et non-philosophie* (Bruxelles-Liege: Pierre Mardaga, 1989), 42 ff.

tariat will not have "values" anymore and will act only according to emergency to save itself from the suffering tormented body and soul.

The proletariat is, let us remind ourselves, everyone who lives on the basis of wage labor and everyone who has to sell his or her labor as a commodity. "Proletariat is recruited from all classes of the population," states the *Communist Manifesto*.[5] Contrary to most criticisms, I would say that the "Occupy Wall Street" slogan, which opposes 99% of the population to the 1%, does have a real addressee. However, it has failed to mobilize hardly 1% of those 99% because we are all bearers of the capitalist philosophy that leads us to believe in what is in fact a religious-moralist premise at the origin of the capitalist world: it is due to our own "inbuilt deficiency" (to be able to succeed) that we have "failed" to become "more like those 1%."

The belief that through wage labor one can "succeed," and that enormous wealth is the natural result of (or reward for) a success of such scale, is what keeps us enslaved in the ruling capitalist logic and paralyses any possibility of revolt. So, the totems of "success," "hard work," and the naturalization of capitalism that elevates its logic to an onto-theological instance of being "the infallible judgment of the 'real' world" against which our worth (not only financial but moral and even ontological) is measured, keeps us entrapped in the philosophical. The urgency to cease the suffering of the tormented body and replace it with joy will act as the real — as "the lived" (Laruelle) and as "the event" (Badiou)—which shall burst asunder the mirror-world of surplus value, that universe of pure abstraction and operations of speculation called capitalism.

I.1. Wage Labor as Abstract Labor and its Realist Alternatives

Wage labor and rented life must be replaced by forms of labor which are not alienated and self-alienating, which are founded upon some materiality, are filled with substance, and are determined by some real in the last instance, but not by the abstraction of labor force. If in the choice of a profession or vocation, the pleasure or the mere feeling more at home with one job rather than another is respected, and the right to it is guaranteed, labor becomes concrete, material, and real, in the sense that one is not alienated from it. It is also real because it is not an abstraction—as in labor force as a cognitive creation, a pure concept—but a tangible reality,

---

[5] Karl Marx and Frederick Engels, "Manifesto of the Communist Party," in Karl Marx and Frederick Engels, *Selected Works*, Vol. 1: 1845-1859 (Moscow: Progress Publishers, 1969), available at https://www.marxists.org/archive/marx/works/1848/communist-manifesto/.

physical and sensuous. In that way, the talk of labor, its economic theorizations and political considerations, will be conditioned and determined in the last instance by the real. In such way, we will not achieve mere theoretical satisfaction of having established a realist discourse. The goal is also practical, as it consists of ensuring that "human resources planning", "life-long learning policies" (such as those of the EU), and other political and scientific operations that shape our realities will be more realistic.

Participation in social production is fundamentally different from wage labor, which is rented participation, as through the process of labor renting itself it schizophrenically splits. It acts as a commodity, albeit being the force that produces objects which become commodities as soon as they are alienated from one's labor and from their use value, and as soon as they turn into numbers (figures, prices). Such contradictions, according to Marx, lead to the preponderance of the tendency that is materially grounded, and as a consequence, to the disappearance of the one which is determined in the last instance by speculation. Materially, in terms of the reality of production, wage labor is force of production. Unilaterally defined, it is the source of commodity creation. Only on the level of the abstract, and only through the process of the fetishization of signification or of the speculation of worth, it is turned into and re-presents itself as commodity. The sheer *physical or sensuous interest* of the human-in-human will eventually thrust against the narrative of wage labor as a measurement of "success" and "dignified life" (both bourgeois concepts that could be radicalized in terms of non-Marxism). The shriek for a bearable life will silence the talk of bourgeois happiness and how it ought to be earned or lost. Participation in social production is the foundation for the survival of a society and its technological development. However, the right to life is a given by nature, and the conatus for survival is the unconditional claim to this right. Therefore, society cannot condition the right to life since it would be a speculative claim against the brute materiality of the struggle for survival. The right to life should be unconditionally granted to every living being—both human and animal—which means sufficient food, housing, heating, and "physical and spiritual wellbeing." Participation in social production should bring rewards which increase what Marx would call physical and spiritual wellbeing. In order to participate in a society, one should be required to participate in the production, according to one's substantive (material) interests, competences, and the sense of "feeling at home" with one's work. However, those who are unable to respond to this requisite should not be deprived of the right to life exercised as "life-increasing" activity or pleasure (Spinoza).

Wage labor is temporary, unstable; in fact, mobility, i.e. the socially and economically enforced compulsion of changing jobs or professions, are the cause of constant stress. One is pressed to constantly treat oneself as insufficiently competent, to constantly train oneself for some new job (that he or she might never get), to acquire new competencies, to even *learn how to love the next job* (and often fail at it), and to fear losing it. The "labor market mobility" in the age of neoliberalism entails doing a literally *alien* job, and maintaining an alienated stance to it (not to "get too attached to it," since one might have to "move on"). Constant instability reinforces the sense of being estranged, de-realized, un-real, and a stranger (often enemy) to oneself. Because of this, capitalism's mode of exploitation is profoundly brutal since it creates self-exploiting subjects of the workforce. Stability of the workplace is the necessary requirement for abolishing wage work as rented life. "Mobility," or the possibility of change in the life-increasing activity aspect (in Spinozian sense), should be made available. Nonetheless, it ought to cease to be imposed through policies of the states of corporate capital, which leaves no space for other options. Let us note that neoliberal labor mobility has a twofold sense: if workers are not mobile, their employers are, *by moving to other corners of the "labor market world."*

Stability is spatial and presupposes attachment to material conditions. The speed of the self-accelerating sheer abstraction that exploits and auto-exploits is radically slowed down by the brute materiality that ensures its stability. Benjamin Noys argues that resistance of the "Occupy" type, which operates with spatial strategies (sit-ins, occupation of public spaces and buildings, etc.), is one that subverts the temporal methodology of the neoliberal capitalist state.[6] A call for occupation of the workplace, as *topos* (of the socio-political realm), and as space in the literal sense, is a resistance strategy that builds well on the new forms of revolt and revolution carried out by "the rebel cities" that David Harvey writes about.[7] Stability or grounding in the materiality of labor provides stability and growth in the real economy as social reproduction, but also as production and technological growth (as means of emancipation of the humankind and of effective protection of other forms of life on the planet). The core of capitalism is the "waging of labor," which is the central mechanism of exploitation. It is also the grounding act of instituting the capitalist and bourgeois universe as one of speculation out of joint. Immanent, realist, or materialist revolt is one against exploitative abstraction of labor that is possible only by way of subjugating, tormenting,

---

[6] Benjamin Noys, "The War of Time: Occupation, Resistance, Communization," *Identities: Journal for Politics, Gender and Culture* 10.1-2 (2013): 83-92.
[7] David Harvey, *Rebel Cities: From the Right to the City to the Urban Revolution* (London: Verso, 2013).

and exploiting the body of the human animal. The revolt of the proletariat should consist of "all classes of the population," or the revolt of the laborers should be directed against the tormented body of the laborer and other animals.

If the source of capitalist exploitation is wage labor that alienates work and its fruits from the worker, the core of capitalist world order consists in some grounding dispossession of humankind (and of other animals too). It is a dispossession from one's work and one's immediate "physical and spiritual" interests, and it is against this form of dispossession that socialism (and communism) revolt in order to offer an alternative to it. A form of re-possession of one's "real," "physical," and "sensuous" labor and its fruits is one of the central goals of Marx's communist vision. Marx is very explicit that the essence of communism is: "reintegration or return of man to himself, the transcendence of human self-estrangement," as well as grasping "the positive essence of private property, and [...] the *human* nature of need."[8] Gaining possession of one's work and its fruits, aligned with one's immediate needs or interests that have "transcended self-alienation," repossessing oneself is the main goal of communism, says Marx. The intimation of this claim is that the idea of possession, and hence, property, needs to be reinvented by recourse to the *chôra* of Marx's concepts.

I.2. Abstraction, Philosophical and Speculative Economies and the Subjugation of the Body

Let us remind ourselves of a passage by Marx, quoted in Chapter 2. Marx describes here the physical reality of the exploited body (and mind) of the wage laborer in the following way:

> [...] the worker becomes ever more exclusively dependent on labour, and on a particular, very one-sided, machine-like labour at that. Just as he is thus depressed spiritually and physically to the condition of a machine and from being a man becomes an abstract activity and a belly, so he also becomes ever more dependent on every fluctuation in market price.[9]

By becoming an abstract activity and a belly, the worker be-

---

[8] Karl Marx, "Third Manuscript: Private Property and Communism," in Karl Marx, *Economic and Philosophical Manuscripts of 1844* (Moscow: Progress Publishers, 1959), available at http://www.marxists.org/archive/marx/works/1844/manuscripts/comm.htm.

[9] Karl Marx, "First Manuscript: Wages of Labor," in Marx, *Economic and Philosophical Manuscripts of 1844*, available at https://www.marxists.org/archive/marx/works/1844/manuscripts/wages.htm.

comes ever more dependent on every fluctuation of market price. The workings of abstraction produce a split and vulnerable self. Vulnerability makes the subject of wage labor dependent on precisely what subjugates it, splits it, and renders it vulnerable—which is the labor market itself. Fluctuation or job instability is therefore the source and the prime mover of exploitation and the deepening sense of suffering. The more vulnerable one is, the more dependent one is on precisely what exploits him or her, and vice versa. The neoliberal acceleration of the Machine of Capital, carried out through measures of absolute specul(ariz)ation of its operations, has deprived labor of all materiality—rendering it pure abstraction or labor force "in general," with "transferable" rather than substantive skills and knowledge. Through its educational policies aligned with the needs of the labor market, the European neoliberal post-nation state aims to ensure mobility from one workplace to another by way of constant re-training and re-education. In this way, precariousness becomes the defining feature of the workforce today, regardless of whether employed or unemployed (the unemployed or the "underemployed" are merely the ever growing "workers reserve army" that Marx wrote of).[10] *Alongside the processes of de-realization of economy, executed through the introduction of the absolute rule of the "finance industry," an unstoppable acceleration of the de-realization of labor has been instituted.*

De-realization invokes a sense of "non-existence," a sense of social invisibility, and fundamental helplessness that induces social-political disempowerment. As a consequence, the army of workers (both active and in reserve) are immobilized as a political and social force in their own right. In immobilization via disempowerment, one should add the sense of confusion with regard to the source of the general state of precariousness affecting the contemporary labor force. By way of the amphibology established between thought and the real, originating from the philosophical decision on what constitutes reality, the worker of the neoliberal and postmodern era is constituted as pure signification (a concept) of abstract labor, which can take on any material form depending on the "dictate of the laws of the labor market." Therefore, she or he becomes convinced that there is no reality beyond the reality of sign and representation, and that material substance is mere material of the higher conceptual reality of "ideas" which molds it. Consequently, the body should endure suffering in the name of

---

[10] Karl Marx, "Relative Diminution of the Variable Part of Capital Simultaneously with the Progress of Accumulation and of the Concentration that Accompanies It," in Karl Marx, *Capital: A Critique of Political Economy*, Vol. I: The Process of Production of Capital (Moscow: Progress Publishers, 1887), available at http://www.marxists.org/archive/marx/works/1867-c1/ch25.htm#S2.

"values," "goals," "lifestyle," and in the name of "self-perfection." Re-education, the search for the "right job," or the constant attempt at yet another job boil down to accepting precariousness as "the call" (of the "natural laws of society") to demonstrate one's abilities and faculties (to survive and "advance" in terms of career).

The capitalist nation-state is constituted by citizens. In it, the citizen's self is constituted as modern, enlightened, and consequently, bourgeois. In the free world of economy, the worker's self is radically individual, autonomous, and endowed with self-mastery. Therefore, exploitation is not an exterior reality to the modern (and post-modern) bourgeois subjectivity of the citizen - it is a sign of one's failure to compete and succeed on the labor market and in the world of capitalist accumulation of wealth. In the last instance, the bourgeois self is constituted as potentially capitalist rather than actually capitalist, and the potential and always already failed capitalist is a member of the proletariat. Hence, the unemployed worker has no outside enemy, seeing himself or herself as the failed capitalist rather than a proletarian. Therefore, there is no class-consciousness among the totality of wage-laborers (which equals the 99% of the "Occupy Wall Street" slogans). For example, instead of revolt, one reacts to unemployment or underemployment with shame. One does not see subjugation and exploitation as the result of some instance of the real, or of an exterior factor (with respect to the real one is in her/his last instance), but rather as the result of one's own lack of capacity to succeed, and therefore of one's lack of "worth" as a person. The myopia of this sort is enabled by capitalism-as-philosophy, i.e. by the speculative postulation of reality that surreptitiously replaces the instance of the real and acts in its stead. Instead of recognizing one's most immediate, physical "interests," one pursues abstractions of "success" and "a worthy self." Therefore, one finds her or himself combating specters of re-presentation, rather than the material force that subjugates him or her. One is radically detached from one's immediate, physical, and material interests to the extent of discarding their alarms as "noise" or mere disturbance of "the inferior instincts" that one needs to transcend in order to succeed.

The materialistic stance of the capitalist subject, embodied by both the wage laborer and the capitalist, is marked by an anorexic treatment of the physical. Namely, the material is indeed the only thing that can make the capitalist subject happy. However, immersing into it without control or allowing it to devour you through pleasure (and pain) renders the material meaningless - "mere matter." It matters when it is fetishized as money, as a trophy wife, as a sculpted (instead of a mere) body, as sex that is not organs and fluids but a representation, or as a home that is not (just) a home but an important element of hyper-stylization of one's life. If the material does not satisfy the fantasized fetishistic expectations, its immediate, unruly, primitive needs are treated as mere defect, and their urgencies are (expected to be) subjected to self-control by the subject.

Capitalist materialism is about an absolute mastery of the mind over the material, it presupposes the hierarchy between matter and mind where the latter is superior to the former. A materialism of this sort is contradictory. Indeed, capitalism is not materialistic, but quite to the contrary: speculation and abstraction rule the physical in an absolute and despotic way. Just as the laborer's body is a tortured body, so is that of the animal, in mass industries, and in nature as a whole. The cruelty of capitalism consists in the capacity to fully rationalize any suffering of the body as well as the relentless exploitation of all organic life. The absolute rule of humanity and its reason is no different than the rule of Hegel's Spirit whose aim is not only the absolute subjugation of Nature, but also its destruction in the name of the reign of the "pure reason." This apocalyptic eschatological vision is explicitly advocated in the *Phenomenology of the Spirit*.[11]

Speculation and operations of thought or of the transcendental (Laruelle) are at the heart of technological progress, of contemporary "management" of economy, and the "governance" of society. Speculation is at the core of the political power. However, in order for these workings of thought to have an effect on the reality, it is necessary that they are materialized, executed through, or upon the physical. In order for them to be *realized*, in order for them to become real, they have to create a material, physical effect. In order to realize the vision of a world of the absolute rule of technology and of pure rationalism, an intervention into the organic is required with the purpose of erasing, re-inventing, and finally substituting the naturally created material with the one which is the product of human appropriation and re-production of matter (both organic and inorganic). The eschatology of technology and the rational mind of enlightenment consist of a vision of the perfect re-production of nature with the paradoxical goal of arriving to the absolute of nature (one that can be executed by the human mind). Within this eschatological vision, the mind is understood in conformity with the Cartesian legacy, i.e. as something not only radically detached from but also opposed to the organic.

As explained in the previous chapters, for Marx, the notions of the physical, sensual, material, and the real are interchangeable. I subscribe to Lacan's and Laruelle's understanding of the real as the effect or modality of reality manifested in the form of trauma or *tuché*. The term *tuché* comes from the ancient Greek word mean-

---

[11] Marx, "Third Manuscript: Private Property and Communism," in Marx, *Economic and Philosophical Manuscripts of 1844*.

ing both "accident" and "encounter." The real "takes place" only in the form of a thrust into and a disruption of the signifying chain. In short, the real is the exteriority to thought, "the out there" to human subjectivity determined in the last instance by language. It is unruly; it lacks form and meaning. It is an unexpected, elemental intervention of "what makes no sense" into the/a universe of sense and meaning and the world. Making sense out of its affects is operating with the re-presentation of the real, not with the real itself. Thus, although workings of thought create effects of the real, when they assume the status of the real, they make no sense and are as elemental as the vulgar real of nature.

Although nature is a reality that can be technically reproduced and intervened upon, it is first and foremost the radical exteriority to thought, regardless of whether we are dealing with "nature proper," or its synthetic technological re-production. The pretension of thought to act in the stead of the real, and in particular of nature, is essentially philosophical and speculative. Therefore, invading nature with reason is analogous to mind's oppressive and exploitative control and subjugation of the body, one based on the old Greek, Christian, and Cartesian dichotomy and hierarchy between body and mind.

Nature, the physical, and the sensuous, are the real in the last instance since they are determined by their being outside of what makes sense, by their being the thrust of *tuché* into the automaton of signification (the human mind). Concepts can also assume the status of the real if they act as an exteriority by virtue of producing material conditions for the thinking subject that seeks to grasp it (in the double sense of the word).

Thus, in order to be a materialist not a rationalist—and a communist, as capitalism is about rationalism rather than materialism—one has to make a metaphysical choice of assigning a different status to the material within the frame of the given dichotomy. Or, following Laruelle, one can dismantle the dichotomy itself as essentially philosophical, or abstract and argue for "dualization"[12] whereby thought and the real are seen in their unilaterality as radically distinct categories. The realist (and materialist) thought succumbs to the authority of the real, rather than to the always already auto-referential universe of philosophy. A truly materialist thought will not be moved by the pretension to fully subjugate the body, but will rather respond to its effects of resistance—to the thrust of irrationality into the translucent sense of abstraction that capitalist bourgeois society consists of. The inferior position of the body in the body-mind hierarchy is what enables the capitalist exploitation of lives in the name of an abstraction. It is for this rea-

[12] François Laruelle, *Philosophie et non-philosophie* (Liege-Bruxelles: Pierre Mardaga 1989), 93–95.

son that a communist revolution to overthrow capitalism entails a process of coming to terms with some metaphysical presuppositions, those that preserve the superior, masterful, and exploitative position of mind or "the Idea." Such choice is political, but also one determined by a realist epistemic stance that is essentially non-philosophical both in the Marxian and Laruellian sense. In the last instance, realist thought succumbs to the authority of the real rather than to a philosophical system.

Nature, the organic, and the bodily, as the exteriority *par excellence* with regard to thought manifested as trauma, is what the realist, materialist, and Marxian thought succumbs to in the last instance, rather than to a philosophy or to a political program (which is the same as philosophy). The ambition to surreptitiously replace the unruly reality (of nature) with a speculative universe which pretends to be the real will inevitably be undercut by a thrust of "what makes no sense," caused by either "ecological catastrophes," by the trauma of the *lived*, or of the real as embodied pain that the human in the last instance is (i.e. by the revolting victim). The "out there" that is presumably material is always already "nature." According to Anthony Paul Smith, thought necessarily presupposes nature as its cognitive regulatory and organizational principle:

> The thought can never become unnatural; it is never not a real idea and what is real is natural. Thought can have real effects, but cannot affect the Real; thought can think the unnatural, but it does not do so unnaturally.[13]

Nature, says Anthony Paul Smith, is one of "the first names of the real." The only real we (meaning us, the humans and our subjectivities) encounter is that which comes from the physical world. The most radical form of transcendental transposition of the realm of "the encountered, physical out-there" is the concept of "nature" in its least scientific, least philosophically informed, radically descriptive (Laruelle), and commonsensical form of "manifest image (Sellars). As any transcendental, nature too potentially engenders its philosophical re-appropriations. The classical, most authoritative, and most enduring philosophical postulation of nature is the one that has produced the hierarchy between the physical (material) and the mind (idea), while simultaneously declaring it (the hierarchy) the foundation of any viable philosophy on any of the two components of the binary. According to this hierarchy, from Aristotle to Descartes, and the Enlightenment to 21st century ideas of sciences and morals, matter/nature is the inferior term in

---

[13] Anthony Paul Smith, *A Non-Philosophical Theory of Nature: Ecologies of Thought* (New York: Palgrave Macmillan, 2013), 15.

the hierarchy. Within the frame of this binary, inferiority seems to function as an invitation to exploitation and subjugation. Hence, nowadays we rarely speak of nature (except in romantic and recreational idioms), but rather of "natural resources" and ecology, whose primary goal is to provide "sustainability" of these resources. When the authoritative discourses of politics and science refer to nature in the second decade of the 21st century, they invoke a speculative entity that perpetuates exploitation in the name of the absolute speculation—contemporary capitalism.

> No, nature is not veiled, but thinking this allows our regional knowledges to think that they can unveil nature, that they can touch and circumscribe nature with thought and thereby either exploit her for our own gain or save her. Our contemporary climate, both in the physical and intellectual sense, is determined by a single force: the neoliberal capitalist ideology that demands everything reduce its value to the quantitative measure of money so that it can produce more of this measure. Nature, though, appears to be purposely deviating from what is accepted as good, proper, or reasonable in capitalist society. Nature itself appears to be refusing to go away, to separate itself off from "culture" and the human person, and insists on inhering to every part of culture and within every human person, and it resists bowing before capitalism's demand, to be measured as something relative rather than the radical condition for any relative measurement.[14]

Exploitation and alienation are made possible by the procedure of alienating nature (or the physical and the material) through speculation, which renders it a resource to the goal of "economic growth," the highest purpose of the totality of human activity in the universe of capitalism. The goal of communism is establishing complete unity of man with nature, argues Marx:

> The *human* aspect of nature exists only for *social* man; for only then does nature exist for him as a *bond* with man—as his existence for the other and the other's existence for him—and as the life-element of human reality. Only then does nature exist as the *foundation* of his own *human* existence. Only here has what is to him his *natural* existence become his *human* existence, and nature become man for him.[15]

[14] Smith, *A Non-Philosophical Theory of Nature*, 14–15.
[15] Marx, "Third Manuscript: Private Property and Communism," in Marx, *Economic and Philosophical Manuscripts of 1844*.

However, it is the "human aspect" of nature which "exists only for social man," and not the nature in itself or "per se" that one establishes unity with. The human aspect of nature is lived by "the social man" in the form of a "bond with men" (Marx)[16]. In this sense, nature is not an object of scientific thought, but rather a material ("physical and sensuous") existence.

Alienation from oneself is alienation from the physical ("natural") bond with fellow "social men." Communism seeks to restore the sense of immediacy, the physicality of this bond, by turning abstraction into the "lived" (Laruelle).

II. The Status of Property in Marx's Texts: An Attempt to Conceptualize Property beyond the Private/Public Binary as conceived by the Modern (and "Post-Modern") Bourgeois State and its Economic Systems

There are two modes of property Marx writes about in *Philosophical and Economic Manuscripts of 1844*: property as such (in linguistic terminology: synchronic conceptualization) and the bourgeois conception of property (property in the historical and material context of capitalist modernity). However, the generic concept of "property" in Marx takes shape and specific determination in a historical and material context. One can derive the genericity of the concept for cognitive purposes. However, the derived concept is not self-sufficient and does not constitute a reality in its own right. Quite the contrary, the real of property is always and necessarily historically determined. The abstraction "property," as a general and ahistorical category, and the tendency to abolish "property in itself," is politically and socially meaningless. "Private property," as conceived in the bourgeois and capitalist state, is what communism seeks to transcend or abolish:

> The antithesis between *lack of property* and *property*, so long as it is not comprehended as the antithesis of *labour and capital*, still remains an indifferent antithesis, not grasped in its *active connection*, in its *internal* relation, not yet grasped as a *contradiction*. It can find expression in this *first* form even without the advanced development of private property (as in ancient Rome, Turkey, etc.). It does not yet *appear* as having been established by private property itself. But labour, the subjective essence of private property as exclusion of property, and capital, objective labour as exclusion of labour, constitute *private property* as

---

[16] Marx, "Third Manuscript: Private Property and Communism," in Marx, *Economic and Philosophical Manuscripts of 1844*.

its developed state of contradiction—hence a dynamic relationship driving towards resolution.[17]

Capital relies on the abstraction of labor and its alienation from the worker. In capitalism, private property is conditioned by the process of alienation of labor. Anti-capitalist struggle seeks to overcome private property that is conditioned by the contradiction of one's labor that is not one's own, to enable the return of work to the worker, to transform (abstract) labor back to work, and to turn private property into possession of one's work and its fruits. Possession and property are distinct categories, the latter being conditioned by legal relations, argues Marx in *Critique of Political Economy*:

> Hegel, for example, correctly takes ownership, the simplest legal relation of the subject, as the point of departure of the philosophy of law. No ownership exists, however, before the family or the relations of master and servant are evolved, and these are much more concrete relations. It would, on the other hand, be correct to say that families and entire tribes exist which have as yet only *possessions* and not *property* [...]. One can conceive an individual savage who has possessions; possession in this case, however, is not a legal relation.[18]

If the communist alternative to private property is common possession (or, in its legal form, common property), community must not be conceived as an abstraction, leaving the individual alienated from what is commonly owned or consumed. Communism is about "reintegration or return of man to himself, the transcendence of human self-estrangement," argued Marx.[19] The sense or the sensuous experience of ownership, or unalienated access to the fruits of human society's production, must belong to the individual not to the society. However, the latter is an impossibility since the society that is not materialized on individual level is abstraction:

The first positive annulment of private property—

---

[17] Marx, "Third Manuscript: Private Property and Communism," in Marx, *Economic and Philosophical Manuscripts of 1844*.
[18] Karl Marx, "Introduction," in Karl Marx, *A Contribution to the Critique of Political Economy*, trans. S.W. Ryazanskaya (London: Lawrence & Wishart, 1971), available at http://www.marxists.org/archive/marx/works/1859/crtique-pol-economy/appx1.htm.
[19] Marx, "Third Manuscript: Private Property and Communism," in Marx, *Economic and Philosophical Manuscripts of 1844*.

crude communism—is thus merely a *manifestation* of the vileness of private property, which wants to set itself up as the *positive community system*. "(2) Communism (α) still political in nature—democratic or despotic; (β) with the abolition of the state, yet still incomplete, and being still affected by private property, i.e., by the estrangement of man. In both forms communism already is aware of being reintegration or return of man to himself, the transcendence of human self-estrangement; but since it has not yet grasped the positive essence of private property, and just as little the *human* nature of need, it remains captive to it and infected by it. It has, indeed, grasped its concept, but not its essence.[20]

Regulation of the commonality of possession, or communal participation in possession, is the organizational backbone of a communist society. The real communist regulation enables immediacy, as it meets what Marx calls *the real interests* of the "physical, spiritual, and sensuous human" (Marx), and thus fulfills the central concern of communism ("reintegration or return of man to himself, the transcendence of human self-estrangement").[21] The Leninist, and its consequent historical derivation of state apparatus, being conceived according to the philosophical authority of the party doctrine, produces even deeper alienation than the bourgeois state; the idea of the proletariat becomes an abstraction and requires philosophical competence in order to be interpreted. By delegating the authority of defining its place and role in society and history to the Party and its ideological masters, i.e. the owners of truths who were endowed with the right to mastering/ruling, the proletariat becomes alienated from its essence, or the substance designated as determined it in the last instance to be a proletarian. The communal participation in possession or access to that which satisfies the proletarian's material and spiritual interests is mediated, controlled, and disciplined by the Party and the state apparatus. The state apparatuses of the so-called communist regimes in the 20th century are an abstraction of the "proletarian will," and only by virtue of this fact do they contradict the definition of communist society as posited by Marx (as shared above). State ownership of production forces and resources are not the same as public ownership (understanding the term "public" in its generic sense, one which can be trans-historically applied).

---

[20] Marx, "Third Manuscript: Private Property and Communism," in Marx, *Economic and Philosophical Manuscripts of 1844*.
[21] Marx, "Third Manuscript: Private Property and Communism," in Marx, *Economic and Philosophical Manuscripts of 1844*.

Marx himself never proposed a specific vision of societal organization that would enable commonality of possession or ownership in the non-bourgeois and non-capitalist sense. Considering that the Leninist vision was materialized as an alienating and oppressive state apparatus, and considering that Marx did not provide a recipe for how to organize, structure, or manage public or communal ownership, it is the task of the communists of the 21st century to conceive of communist societal (and political-economic) organization/s in accordance with its own historical context/s. With the core of the communist vision being "overcoming of alienation," commonality should be conceived in terms of providing a sense and materiality of individual ownership over something common or communal. One can take the example of Wikipedia: the reality that it is owned by everyone who desires to participate in its ownership is enabled by the actual sense that he or she can claim it as their own, along with billions of other people on the planet. Therefore, instead of abolishing property and all forms of individual ownership, the meaning of ownership and property should be reinvented along the lines of the main Marxian concern—transcending alienation. The notion of "private" invites a communist reinvention too—reconceptualization in the sense of providing an individual sense of participation in the commons, an immediate and non-alienating experience of having the right to consume and produce, and a sense of immediacy which is a sense of being at home with it, of "owning" it, and "being intimate" with it. This type of experience offers a sense of privacy, or privacy in its ownership. It is opposite to a sense of dispossession, which is identical to that of alienation. In line with Marx's definition of the main goal of communism, private ownership can be reinvented as ownership, and privacy in ownership, which is not based on exploitation, commodification, and private property, as opposed to commons and wage labor.

The Communist Manifesto advocates abolition of the family. However, that does not mean that it calls for the abolition of all forms of family or kinship, only of the bourgeois one. Analogically, it also advocates abolition of private property, but that does not mean that it calls for the abolishment of all forms of ownership, or of all forms of privacy or individuality with respect to ownership. It calls upon transcendence of those forms of private property that are based in exploitation and the alienation of human nature. To put it differently, it envisions and calls for the establishment of a new form of ownership, one in alignment with nature representing the appropriation of "human essence," which is in its last instance material:

> *Communism* as the *positive* transcendence of *private property* as *human self-estrangement*, and therefore as the real *appropriation* of

the *human* essence by and for man; communism therefore as the complete return of man to himself as a *social* (i.e., human) being—a return accomplished consciously and embracing the entire wealth of previous development. This communism, as fully developed naturalism, equals humanism, and as fully developed humanism equals naturalism; it is the *genuine* resolution of the conflict between man and nature and between man and man—the true resolution of the strife between existence and essence, between objectification and self-confirmation, between freedom and necessity, between the individual and the species. Communism is the riddle of history solved, and it knows itself to be this solution.[22]

To prohibit the immediate sense of individual ownership of the process of production is alienating, and against "human nature" as defined by Marx. The goal of communism is "fully developed naturalism." Mediation of ownership through structured collectivity that is regulated by law, law/legality being the founding determination of property, is irrevocably alienating. Therefore, the individual sense of ownership of the process of production must be enabled by the regulating apparatus of a society based on the principle of the commonality of resources and social reproduction. Communist society is an eschatological vision of radical transcendence of human estrangement. Hence, an abstract social self enabled by the self-negating or self-nullifying individual subject would be in contradiction with the central promise of the communist horizon.

In such a case, one would face once again, although in a reverse or perverse form, capitalist ownership where the collective establishes itself as the "universal capitalist," and the individual subject must transcend alienation through its realization as a "species being."[23] The human as a species being is fundamentally a social being, argues Marx. Thus, a non-alienated individual is the basis for a non-alienating society, and vice versa; the non-alienating society enables a non-alienated life for the human individual. The dialectics at stake is one that we find in Foucault—the subject enables a certain societal structure and discourse-power, just as much as that very structure conditions the subject. The dilemma on the primacy of "the doer and the deed" is a false one. It is a collective dynamism of creating subjectivities that take place outside the dualistic logic that intimates the necessity of demiurgic active subjectivity, and the sterile passive objectivity of the created. If we look

[22] Marx, "Third Manuscript: Private Property and Communism," in Marx, *Economic and Philosophical Manuscripts of 1844*.
[23] Marx, "Third Manuscript: Private Property and Communism," in Marx, *Economic and Philosophical Manuscripts of 1844*.

at this process from a non-philosophically unilateral perspective, each individual is determined in the last instance as species-member, permitting him/her to act as both individual and social being at the same time, without temporal priority of either of the two modalities of existence. Hence, ownership of both production and its fruits (as well as the access to their consumption) ought to be both individual and social, in line with the following principle of communism conceived as the "*genuine* resolution of the conflict between man and nature and between man and man—the true resolution of the strife between existence and essence, between objectification and self-confirmation, between freedom and necessity, between the individual and the species."[24]

In Volume 1 of *Capital*, Marx argues that not all private property is the same, saying, "as these private individuals are labourers or not labourers, private property has a different character."[25] "Parceling of soil and of the productive forces of a society" is the problematic aspect of petty industry and pre-capitalist agriculture that is based on the private ownership of the means of production by the individual laborer. Marx advocates full re-socialization of the laborer's ownership of their means of production after the inevitable historical stage of capitalism has passed, arguing that such a process:

> [...] does not re-establish private property for the producer, but gives him individual property based on the acquisition of the capitalist era: *i.e.*, on cooperation and the possession in common of the land and of the means of production. The transformation of scattered private property, arising from individual labour, into capitalist private property is, naturally, a process, incomparably more protracted, violent, and difficult, than the transformation of capitalistic private property, already practically resting on socialized production, into socialized property. In the former case, we had the expropriation of the mass of the people by a few usurpers; in the latter, we have the expropriation of a few usurpers by the mass of the people.[26]

Here, Marx argues that individual property is distinct from private property, but also that communist individual property

---

[24] Karl Marx, "Historical Tendency of Capitalist Accumulation," in Marx, *Capital*, Vol. I, available at http://www.marxists.org/archive/marx/works/1867-c1/ch32.htm.
[25] Marx, "Historical Tendency of Capitalist Accumulation," in Marx, *Capital*, Vol. 1.
[26] Marx, "Historical Tendency of Capitalist Accumulation," in Marx, *Capital*, Vol. 1.

does not entail ownership of the means of production. Land and means of production should be subject to "possession in common." In an imagined communist universe, individual property persists in the *mode* of commonality, or in the substance of active participation in the common sense and reality of ownership.

The *chôra* of Marx's text invites us to invent modes of possession of commonality that will not erase the individual sense and reality of ownership, and will be based on non-alienated labor (by way of non-alienated relations to the means of production). Particularly after 1989, we know that we have to reinvent the communist state. We also know that the mere appropriation of the means and resources of production by the state guarantees neither commonality nor transcendence of workers' alienation from their labor as the goal of communism, as stated by Marx. If we want the reestablishment of the "communist horizon"[27] in the 21st century to be one executed in accordance with the real, rather than with or as philosophy, we ought to proceed by way of aligning (in the last instance) with the dictate of the real, rather than with the inner logic of Marx's *opus*.

III. Political Aspects of the Economy of Commonalities: The Acceleration of 21st Century Capitalism Toward a Society with Free Associations of Producers

III.1. Dispelling the Illusion of the Neoliberal Weak State

The organization of social production beyond the principle of private property qua property based on wage labor needs to be conceived in terms of a given historical and material context. There is no single form of commonality, beyond historical context and the real conditions that it generates. Any form of commonality that transcends the praxis of historically determined conditioning circumstances are an abstraction, and idea hovering independently from the material universe. In the first decade of the 21st century, we possess active memory of the reign and demise of "the communist states" of the mid 20th century in Eastern and Central Europe. By inertia, we tend to imagine the state-owned commons of those states as the model of socialist commonality in ownership.

If we submit to the dictate of the real of the material and immaterial conditions of our contemporaneity, the concept of commonality that we would generate would follow the "syntax of the real" as the conditioning of its possibilities. We live in an era of accelerated capitalism, in capital's "bubbles" and "financial crises," which, as we already tried to demonstrate, exist in an almost par-

---

[27] J Jodi Dean, *The Communist Horizon* (London: Verso Books, 2012).

allel fashion to the real economy of the deregulating neoliberal politico-economic doctrine. The alleged deregulation of the neoliberal economy is in fact a product of a meticulous scientifically, ideologically, politically, and technocratically elaborated methodology of control, masquerading as the manifestation of the anarchic natural laws of the free market economy. We live in an era in which states bailout banks with the money collected through taxes paid by wage laborers. The "weak state" of neoliberalism is stronger and more economically disciplining and socially ruthless than any other form of a bourgeois state that we have witnessed in the second half of the 20th century. In addition to the bank bailouts by the state, let us note that "austerity measures" are one of the most prominent features of the post-2008 economy in Europe.

In short, there is no such thing as a natural or apolitical economy. The economy is always already political, as it is the economy's material core of power, control, and its main mechanisms—i.e. exploitation and oppression. It is no less so in the era of neoliberalism, a time in which we witness the divorce between capitalism and democracy. The divorce is scandalous as we see totalitarian states, such as China, Russia, and Turkey as the new economic superpowers, ever more superior to the West, being the EU and the US. Western countries also are executing a split between democracy and capitalism, nonetheless one that is less scandalously ostensible. Their means of state controlled economy, whose policies do not require and moreover prevent the possibility of democratic expression of endorsement or refusal on the part of the citizens, consists in the measures of "austerity cuts," "market oriented education," rising gender and social inequality, and the sacrifice of the basic human freedoms in the name of "security" in an era of "war against terrorism" that has lasted for more than a decade. *To believe in the story of the weak state as a victim of the "elemental forces" of capitalism implies a prior belief in the narrative of the naturalness of the economic laws (of capitalism).*

In order to lay the foundations of a different economy, one that is *not* based on wage labor and the exploitation of human life and nature, but rather on action in accordance with their resources, we must rethink the concept of the state in a radical way, one structurally different from the modern bourgeois state. If the structure originating in the bourgeois state is preserved, it will mean that the determination in the last instance is still the same. In order to arrive to a determination in the last instance of a non-exploitative, non-wage-labor-based social order where the determination is affected by the real, we must first arrive to the generic core of the notion of the state, and more specifically of the modern state. As soon as we determine the generic term of "the state," we can radicalize it by letting it be determined by the effects of the real. The generic notion, isolated from the *chôra* of the transcendental material that is offered by modern philosophies originating in the Enlightenment, should be used as the minimal transcendental description for the determining effect (or "symptom") of the real.

III.2. Auto-acceleration of Capitalism as Speculation and its Political Infrastructure

According to Marx in Volume 3 of *Capital*, the inherent laws of the capitalist political and economic order will nourish and exacerbate the contradiction between pure speculation as the primary mode of operation of capitalism and the instance of the material it aims to control and exploit. Speculation out of joint will assume a life of its own, detached from the material possession of capital as private property or as simply having actual money. Speculative capital, the capital with which the finance industry operates today, is potential money, pure speculation. Its potentiality derives from investments of mere estimations of the worth of third persons' material property and assets. It is the association of investors and clients, creditors and debtors, the networks they create, and the financial fluxes that such networks navigate, that create financial growth and its economic (side) effects. Marx writes:

> The capital, which in itself rests on a social mode of production and presupposes a social concentration of means of production and labour-power, is here [stock exchange market] directly endowed with the form of social capital (capital of directly associated individuals) as distinct from private capital, and its undertakings assume the form of social undertakings asdistinct from private undertakings. It is the abolition of capital as private property within the framework of capitalist production itself.[28]

Contemporary finance capital, or the so called finance industry, relies and profits from the operations of circulation as a process *per se* and as tautology, divorced from any grounding in the material basis of capital.

I have explained the process in more detail in the previous pages of this book, not only in theoretical terms, but also in terms of evidence related to the post 2008 crisis in the US and henceforth globally. I also presented data, derived from the US Government commissioned report on the crisis, pointing out the absurd fact that the greatest giants of the finance industry had been op-

---

[28] Karl Marx, "Interest and Profit of Enterprise," in Karl Marx, *Capital: A Critique of Political Economy*, Vol. 3: The Process of Capitalist Production, ed. Frederick Engels (New York: International Publishers, 1894), available at http://www.marxists.org/archive/marx/works/1894-c3/ch23.htm.

erating with virtually no capital investment of their own. Their "capital" had been the "information," "knowledge," and political support and legitimation—an engagement of speculation that the US government report on the crisis termed more than once as swindling.[29] According to Marx, such a development is necessary and inevitable as the last stage of capitalism:

> This is the abolition of the capitalist mode of production within the capitalist mode of production itself, and hence a self-dissolving contradiction, which prima facie represents a mere phase of transition to a new form of production. It manifests itself as such a contradiction in its effects. It establishes a monopoly in certain spheres and thereby requires state interference. It reproduces a new financial aristocracy, a new variety of parasites in the shape of promoters, speculators and simply nominal directors; a whole system of swindling and cheating by means of corporation promotion, stock issuance, and stock speculation. It is private production without the control of private property.[30]

This stage is metastatic for capitalism, ensuing into the greatest imaginable contradiction that will lead to self-dissolution, says Marx.

Post-2008 finance capitalism is one of perpetual crisis, whereas, as Jacques Rancière says, crisis cannot be a permanent pathological state as, by definition, it is not permanent. Instead, it is the "robust health system" of exploitation presented as illness to the "ignorant ones" or to the exploited (those who can be convinced that they are "ill" rather than exploited).[31] What our contemporary media and corporate political powers call "crisis" seems to be, by all of its constitutive characteristics, the final stage of capitalism which Marx describes as "self-dissolving." It unveils the reality of economic production and social and technological progress as one unfolding virtually independently from the "material basis" (monetarily re-presented materiality) of private capital.

The acceleration process, which is bound to happen through what Marx called "the credit system," the ever growing distance between actual paying and buying of a commodity, and the possibility of an ever expanding "intermission" of the credit period,

---

[29] Financial Crisis Inquiry Commission (FCIC), *The Financial Crisis Inquiry Report: Final Report of the National Commission on the Causes of the Financial and Economic Crisis in the United States* (Washington, DC: U.S. Government Publishing Office, 2011), available at http://www.gpo.gov/fdsys/pkg/GPO-FCIC/content-detail.html
[30] Marx, "Interest and Profit of Enterprise," in Marx, *Capital*, Vol. 3.
[31] Jacques Rancière, "Time, Narration and Politics," *Identities: Journal for Politics, Gender and Culture: Identities* 11.1 (2014): 13.

divulges the spectrality of capital, money, and private property. Acceleration through the "credit system" as the final stage of capitalism is announced and elaborated by Marx in Volume III, Chapter 5 of *Capital*. As the US Government Report on the 2008 financial crisis shows, Wall Street CEO's do not have to invest any *real* or *actual* private property, and practically no capital of theirs has to be invested in order to initiate, manage, and profit from an investment project. Quite the contrary, it is the private property of the poor that had been invested and then defaulted as the post 2007 crisis occurred. By no material investment of one's own investment, "industrialists" create an unstoppable growing capital that enables them and government to control society as the highest form of politico-economic power. The illusion of capital's materiality and material property, serving as the basis for an economy, has become apparent through the financial speculation whose final form becomes sheer swindling. Albeit aiming at pure profit and exploitation of the poor only, the crisis has also and unwittingly shown that the "emperor had been naked" for quite some time—that capital as the material and real basis of economic processes is a mirage. On the basis of this particular contradiction, the "stock exchange managers" have managed to amass most of the material resources for themselves.

Acceleration is immanent to capitalism. Capitalism is unstoppably accelerated by the inherent laws of speculation itself, and therefore that of de-materialization.

> On one hand, the acceleration is technical; for example, with the same magnitude and number of actual turnovers of commodities for consumption, a smaller quantity of money or money tokens performs the same service. This is bound up with the technique of banking. On the other hand, credit accelerates the velocity of the metamorphoses of commodities, and thereby the velocity of money circulation. [...] Acceleration by means of credit, of the individual phases of circulation or the metamorphosis of commodities, and later the metamorphosis of capital, and with it an acceleration of the process of reproduction in general. (On the other hand, credit helps to keep the acts of buying and selling apart longer, and serves thereby as a basis for speculation.) Contraction of reserve funds may be viewed in two ways: as a reduction of the circulating medium on the one hand, and on the other, as a reduction of that part of capital which must always exist in the form of money.[32]

---

[32] Karl Marx, "The Role of Credit in Capitalist Production," in Marx, *Capital*, Vol. 3, available at http://www.marxists.org/archive/marx/works/1894-c3/ch23.htm.

One does not need the enactment of a "process of acceleration" of capitalism as a form of resistance aimed at its demise, as the "Accelerationist Manifesto" argues,[33] simply because it is a process generated by capitalism itself. Acceleration does not only take place in the form of finance capital, but also in the area of material production, i.e. in technological-militaristic development. The unstoppable development of the means of production, which is also the means of exploitation of the human species, is constantly accelerated. This is technological development. Technological development is subject to private property, capital invested in it, and the material conditions for it; its inventions are in the possession of capitalist oligarchs exclusively. The imagined political revolution via technological acceleration requires a reversed model of ownership and reinvention of the social role of technological development. In order to achieve these communist goals, following the model of associations of producers advocated by Marx, the technological processes, which are physically (really or "materially") grounded in the individuals who innovate, should be appropriated by the actual producers. As a consequence, this will lead to a replacement of the spectrality and superfluity of capital (money) by real and tangible social re-production.

However, politics in the strict sense is far more complex than economics. It enacts the totality of the relations in a society. That is why the political horizon cannot be reduced to a shift in economic production and ownership. It needs to be invented in accordance with the principle of radical sociality of production as the central economic fundament, as well as with the political (and metaphysical) goal of transcending the dualism of "the belly and the abstract activity" (Marx).

In capitalism, the product of a social process, i.e. of an "association of producers" of commodities, consists of use value and surplus value, or in the case of the finance industry, of surplus value only. It is claimed as property by a handful of people coordinating the social process, including both the political and the economic reality. In other words, capitalism, in particular in its neoliberal form, is not so much about the material possession of what is potentially capital, but about the capacity and entitlement to assign monetary value, and hence, the status of capital (and for that matter, of commodity as well). This is political capacity and entitlement.

In what Marx announces as the late stage of capitalism, i.e. in finance capitalism, the process of signification—of turning a ma-

---

[33] Alex Williams and Nick Srnicek, "#Accelerate: Manifesto for an Accelerationist Politics," *Critical Legal Thinking* (weblog), May 14, 2013, http://criticallegalthinking.com/2013/05/14/accelerate-manifesto-for-an-accelerationist-politics/.

terial, physical good into market value or commodity—is mainly carried out through mere "swindling," as mentioned in the US report on the post 2008 financial crisis. In this process, the "private ownership of property" has been proven to be "just ownership" as Marx predicted—a mere instance of the material to be exploited by the "stock exchange managers" (Marx). As the essentially speculative nature of the capitalist economy has accelerated, the central contradiction has moved to an extreme. According to Marx, the contradiction taken *in extremis* must be resolved by self-dissolving the impossible, unsustainable, contradicting couple. If the unsustainable and bubbled up speculative aspect of the contradiction culminates, if it exacerbates the fissure with the real and the physical that it has introduced *in principio*, it will founder as the real starts to "act on its own," escaping the control of philosophy (= ideology of capitalism). Unruly as it is, thanks to its brutal, physical force, or/and the force of the real, which can include material actions carried out by inanimate agencies, it will disperse the ruling webs of meaning, or the existing universe and estimation of values. Such a process would lead to the self-dissolution of the founding binary of capitalism, because *the reality is constituted by, grounded in, and conditioned by social process, rather than capital investment (in the form of actual monetary assets)*. Materiality of contemporary reality lies in society, in its physicality and effects of a conditioning real, rather than in the symbolism of money.

III.3. Reversing the Self-dissolving Binary

Following Marx's prescriptions, if and when the above takes place, we will be called upon to build a vision of materiality, sociality, and socialism on the material or real basis of the determination in the last instance of the existing and most profitable economic models. This ought to be done by recourse to their materialist re-volution, i.e. by way of arriving at the material/physical determination in the last instance of social representation. The goal of such procedure would be to ground the economic models subject to revolutionary reversal in the material qua real, and condition them by it, i.e. by their material determination in the last instance.

This result of the ultimate development of capitalist production is a necessary transitional phase towards the reconversion of capital into the property of producers, although no longer as private property of the individual producers, but rather as the property of associated producers or outright social property. On the other hand, the stock company is a transition towards the conversion of all functions of in the reproduction process that still remain linked with capitalist property into mere functions of associated producers, or into social functions.[34]

Divested from any real, material, or physical base, divested from a base that maintains its connection with the material via the proxy of investment capital, the model of production dominated by the finance industry unravels the economy's fundamental sociality. Let us remind ourselves of the US Government's report on the post 2008 financial crisis, which notes and documents that the crisis was provoked by the fact that investment giants were operating with virtually no capital of their own. Investment mortgage backed funds or bank crediting were *de facto* made possible by clients' investments, i.e. assets that were at risk to be defaulted. In line with Marx's vision of the last, most developed, and metastatic stage of capitalism, we will call the latter "mere capital owners" (Marx), whereas the true capitalists are those who "manage" the funds without investing any of their material property. He writes:

> Transformation of the actually functioning capitalist into a mere manager or, administrator of other people's capital, and of the owner of capital into a mere owner, a mere money, is capitalist [sic]. Even if the dividends that which they receive include the interest and the profit of enterprise, *i.e.*, the total profit (for the salary of the manager is, or should be, simply the wage of a specific type of skilled labour, whose price is regulated in the labour-market like that of any other labour), this total profit is henceforth received only in the form of interest, *i.e.*, as mere compensation for owning capital that now is entirely divorced from the function in the actual process of reproduction, just as this function in the person of the manager is divorced from ownership of capital. Profit thus appears (no longer only that portion of it, the interest, which derives its justification from the profit of the borrower) as a mere appropriation of the surplus-labour of others, arising from the conversion of means of production into capital, *i.e.*, from their alienation vis-à-vis the actual producer, from their antithesis as another's property to every individual actually at work in production, from manager down to the last day-labourer. In stock companies the function is divorced from capital ownership, hence also labour is entirely divorced from ownership of means of production and surplus-labour.[35]

The Report of the Inquiry Committee on the 2008 financial crisis confirms this projection to be true, and provides ample evidence for it:

[34] Marx, "Interest and Profit of Enterprise," in Marx, *Capital*, Vol. 3.
[35] Marx, "Interest and Profit of Enterprise," in Marx, *Capital*, Vol. 3.

In the years leading up to the crisis, too many financial institutions, as well as too many households, borrowed to the hilt, leaving them vulnerable to financial distress or ruin if the value of their investments declined even modestly. For example, as of 2007, the five major investment banks—Bear Stearns, Goldman Sachs, Lehman Brothers, Merrill Lynch, and Morgan Stanley—were operating with extraordinarily thin capital. By one measure, their leverage ratios were as high as 40 to 1, meaning for every $40 in assets, there was only $1 in capital to cover losses.[36]

Those who capitalize on an investment and those who extract immense profit do not in fact own the material basis for it. What they own is a legally designated status to operate and profit from someone else's private property. Once this becomes obvious, what remains to be done is that someone finally shouts, "the emperor is naked," or at least starts behaving like it. What gives life to the finance industry is the will of "the mere owners of capital" (the exploited ones) to enter into associations that create profit. These processes are fundamentally social. Only a purely social process can enable the usurpation of the real by speculation. In order to overcome the alienation created by such usurpation, which foregrounds exploitation of the bodies of human and non-human animals, one ought to seek the purely material—as the real, physical or practical, and "material," in Marx's sense—grounding of the social.

III.4. The Material or Non-speculative Grounding of the Social

Sociality is a linguistic and communicative reality, its means are of language. It is fundamentally subjectivity. Its radical subjectivity is that which admits the jarring difference between the Laruellian "Stranger," the inevitable gesture of the auto-alienation of the real as the fundament of subjectivity formation, and the real. The radical subjectivity is defined by its anteriority to any philosophical ambition to reconcile the two instances by way of usurping the real, a gesture executed by virtue of establishing an amphibology between the real and the "meaning" (language, subjectivity, truth).

Philosophy, regardless of its inner plurality, can be seen as a monolithic phenomenon in the following sense—it inevitably establishes an equation between the real and thought. Even when it declares an insurmountable split between the two, even when it declares the real to be inaccessible, as in the case of the post-Kantian

---

[36] FCIC, *The Financial Crisis Inquiry Report*, xix.

critical legacy, it still thinks in terms of the equation. Namely, by relegating the real into the realm of the unthinkable, the inaccessible to thought, it commits a "fuite en avance (preemptive escape) into fiction," resulting into instituting language (thought/"fiction"/ the Stranger) as the only form of reality that thought should be interested in and aspire to understand.[37] Thereby, the philosophical affirmation of the irreconcilable split between the real and thought, and of the real's radical indifference to thought's aspirations, remains within the perennial philosophical equation rendering the real reducible to "truth," i.e. to thought. This result is brought about precisely by the reversal of the equation. Namely, through the gesture of declaring the real non-existent, being that it is non-existent for and to us, the philosophical thought of the post-Kantian turn assigns to language the status of the real and perpetuates the same amphibology.[38]

Consequently, in order to determine the material grounding of sociality in the last instance, i.e. in order to establish its determination in the last instance as determination in terms of the real, one ought to avoid philosophical circularity of thought. With the aim of achieving this goal, we shall apply the non-philosophical method of arriving to a concept that is radically descriptive, i.e. minimally transcendental in its identification of the affect of the real that determines it in the last instance.[39] Such posture of thought is fundamentally scientific, says Laruelle. Scientific thought is primitive and naive insofar as it aims to be descriptively exhaustive but does not institute a "truth" of the real, nor does it deal with its "essence."[40] Describing exteriority, its locations, its operations, its effects (on the environment, including the humans), and arriving to an elaborate description is what scientific thought aspires to do.

> Philosophy will always look for and posit science too late—at the end of its 'reflection,' at the end of its 'project' of objectivity, at the end of its 'dialectic', and in general at the end of the transcendence that founds all of its techniques. Now, it is precisely transcendence that science excludes, at least from the relation (of non-relation) that it 'maintains' in the last instance with the real. Hence, its naivety, its unreflectiveness, its realism, its 'blindness,' which is so insupportable to philosophical ob-jectification that the latter

---

[37] Laruelle, *Philosophie et non-philosophie*, 231.
[38] Katerina Kolozova, *The Cut of the Real: Subjectivity in Poststructuralist Philosophy* (New York: Columbia University Press, 2014), 1.
[39] Laruelle, *Introduction au non-marxisme*, 47.
[40] François Laruelle, *From Decision to Heresy: Experiments in Non-Standard Thought* (Falmouth, UK/New York: Urbanomic/Sequence Press, 2012), 98.

never stops denigrating them, reducing them, or falsifying them—this is what goes by the name of 'epistemology', and is the very epistemo-logos in every epistemology. [41]

To define the "essence" of human existence in philosophical terms is to commit violence against the physical (or the "material" in the Marxist or non-philosophical sense). To place it in the realm of abstraction or "pure value" is to formulate it as a *surplus value*. The philosophical determination in the last instance of the human species is no different from the capitalist one. A materialist determination of the human based on Marx's conception of materialism without philosophy, i.e. "scientific" materialism, is one that views the instance of the mental also materialistically. Therefore, if the fundamental interest of the proletariat is social, the form of sociality that the "communist horizon" postulates as its goal is one that would be materially determined by a sense of wellbeing. It will consist of what Marx calls "spiritual satisfaction," combined and in no contradiction with the bodily. Let us remind ourselves one more time that Marx argues that the true goal of communism is the transcendence of human alienation created by the body/mind dichotomy.[42] The "spiritual" necessarily materializes itself as a bodily sensation:

> That man's physical and spiritual life is linked to nature means simply that nature is linked to itself, for man is a part of nature.[43]

The material that Marx is concerned with is that of the physical, of what can suffer or sense pleasure, or in other words, the material of the organic. In the last instance, praxis is also determined by the physical. The communist emancipation is an emancipation of the physical from the tyranny of the Spirit detached from and opposed to the material or the real. It can be reduced to the hierarchically superior constituent of the archaic binary of the body and mind, or matter and idea. It also entails emancipation of the spiritual, which suffers from the alienation and the split between the spiritual and physical production The spiritual suffers insofar as it is an abstract ruling the physical turned into an object, treated as if it was an inanimate matter. It suffers from its own

---

[41] Laruelle, *From Decision to Heresy*, 99-100.
[42] Marx, "Third Manuscript: Private Property and Communism," in Marx, *Economic and Philosophical Manuscripts of 1844*.
[43] Karl Marx, "First Manuscript: Estranged Labor," in Marx, *Economic and Philosophical Manuscripts of 1844*, available at http://www.marxists.org/archive/marx/works/1844/manuscripts/labour.htm.

deprivation of physical sensation, of the death of the physical that it contains in order to be an abstraction. Therefore, technological progress and its acceleration, in communist terms, can be emancipating so long as they are emancipating the subjugated physical and nature. A society of emancipated bodies and minds, a society that has transcended the split and hierarchy between the two, can create and sustain an economy based on the "free associations of producers." The communist concept of economy operates only by virtue of suspending the hierarchy of the "higher good" (an abstraction) over the physical, including the "higher good" of communism and its economy of "free associations." As long as they produce the division of "the belly and the abstract activity," they are not communist.[44]

A communist producer is not alienated from his or her work and its fruits. Therefore, in some sense, communism offers a sense of possession or ownership for every member of society. In order for this "sense of possession" to be material, it has to be realized physically through the bodies of the members of the society. Therefore, in order for communism to be communal it also has to be very individualistic, as each *body* in a society must vouch for it. The idea that the individual must suffer in the name of a common good is absurd (from a materialist point of view, meaningless) and one never argued for by Marx. If so, the common good would become a purpose in itself, a self-serving and auto-referential goal. Hence, it would become an abstraction, detached from the physical experiences of the bodies of a society (not the "social body," as that is yet another abstraction).

In short, by the very logic of Marx's argument, the opposition between the individual and the common would be untenable. Also, it is something Marx never argued for. His critique of the private property is historical, and therefore concerns its bourgeois and/or capitalist form. An argument in favor of sacrificing the individual wellbeing in the name of an abstract higher good is one of martyrdom.

Martyrdom is a theological and philosophical value, not a communist one. Communism is radically democratic. The Leninist and post-Leninist legacy of communism has instituted it as a form of Abrahamic theology, of self-sacrifice and sacrifices, of martyrdom and physical suffering in the name of a grand idea. The theology of this tradition, i.e. the Judeo-Christian and Islamic theology of self-sacrifice, is hateful of democracy in the sense that Jacques Rancière writes of "the hatred of democracy."[45] It is hateful of the idea that everyone is equally competent enough to partici-

---

[44] Marx, "First Manuscript: Wages of Labor," in Marx, *Economic and Philosophical Manuscripts of* 1844.
[45] Jacques Rancière, *The Hatred of Democracy* (London: Verso, 2006).

pate in the building of a just society. It is also hateful of the bodily, of individuality as linked to a mortal body, and its finality vis-à-vis the immortality of the great idea. Such structure of a world (in Larulle's sense, a universe of language which is no less material or real, i.e. a universe determined by the real) is fundamentally religious, and more specifically, Abrahamic. Contrary to this, Marx's idea of commonality is profoundly individualistic, as the idea of equality is one materially established among the individuals in a society, rather than a detached, self-sufficient, or ubiquitous abstraction. As far as property is concerned, commonality should create a reality that is not only perceived, but also experienced—not only as collective, but also as individual—by each and every individual in a society.

The free associations of producers collectively hold possession of the means of production that originate in the commons of all products and forms of access to natural resources. The commons should effectively be equally and directly accessible to every-*body* in a society. The very logic of the structure of a community should determine the accessibility of the commons, as well as the collective or desired contributions to their creation, instead of coerced ones. It should be fundamentally democratic by way of enabling everyone to contribute equally to its re-production, and also by having unlimited access to the use of its products. The products are not commodities, as the surplus value is out of the equation. It is a radically different economic model. At the dusk of capitalism, in the zone of the internet, communities appear that constitute commonality and produce common goods simultaneously. Their products are not final, they do not offer objects that can be manipulated, separated from the community, or commodified. Instead, they enable a process of continuous production. The mechanisms of control are set as internal rules of its productivity, determined in the last instance by a radically democratic concept of knowledge, which is one affected by the immanence of knowledge. The real of knowledge immanently affects the program of its production by allowing it to be constantly generated by the operations of knowledge as real or a matter in its own right, rather than by the philosophical agenda of a group of people who would programmatize the "development" of the community and its production. The mechanisms of control rely precisely on contradiction, conflicting knowledge or views, which are resolved in a way that is more a matter of craft than political power. Anonymity, in the sense of suspension of "auctoritas," is the mode of operation of the creative online communities. The anonymity at issue is not an effacement of the individual, but quite to the contrary, it results from the multitude of individuals that participate in it. The functioning of such a community and its production is fundamentally social, where the social is "superposed" (as in quantum theory) with the individual.

The analogy of superposition taken from Laruelle's non-standard philosophy (a term more often used in the latest stage of non-philosophy), and inspired by quantum theory, serves to enable us to understand the fundamentally social nature of the individual and its reverse, not as a paradox but as two realities that can be viewed unilaterally. The fact that they are viewed unilaterally does not mean that one does not affect the other as its real foregrounding and its determination in the last instance. As questions of temporality are not relevant for our discussion, we are neither interested in the issues of "simultaneity" of both realities, nor in the issues of "sequentiality." It is of no relevance to us whether the individual or the society comes first, neither in the temporal nor in the axiological sense. What matters is that the social constitutes a real in its own right, as does the human-in-human, and that one conditions the other by immanently affecting it.

Only in community does each individual have the means of cultivating his gifts in all directions; therefore, only in the community is personal freedom possible. In the previous substitutes for the community (e.g., in the State), personal freedom has existed only for the individuals who developed as part of the ruling class, and only insofar as they were individuals of that class.[46]

The relations of the two realities ought to be regulated in a way that enables the wellbeing of the bodies that constitute the society as its communist determination in the last instance. Whether the individual engenders society, or the other way around, is a fundamentally philosophical question, one of assigning values in the axiological sense that boils down to theology. The question of the eventual "superposition" of the two realities, in line with its conceptualization in quantum theory, would be a philosophical one. Exploring this issue would be a self-indulging, purely speculative, and auto-referential project, as it is of no direct relevance for the social praxis that is subject to our study. It is inoperative with regard to the project of creating a society that enables equality and wellbeing for every-body, and is therefore irrelevant for the subject matter of this study. Methodological questions in sciences are determined by the subject matter (or "the material") of research. The subject matter in our case is "a transcendental material" that is in its last instance linguistic, namely the political, and is determined by a real that has its own intrinsic laws. The real is not an abstraction. It requires a language of universality. However, universality is not the same as generality. The concept of superposition borrowed

---

[46] Karl Marx, "Feuerbach: Opposition of the Materialist and Idealist Outlooks," in Karl Marx and Frederick Engels, *The German Ideology* (Moscow: Progress Publishers, 1968), available at https://www.marxists.org/archive/marx/works/1845/german-ideology/ch01.htm.

directly from quantum theory operates as a generalization, as it is not the product of a radicalization of a singular and unilaterally postulated real.

5: Technology, the Body, and the Materialist Determination in the Last Instance of the Communist Society of "Cyborgs"

I. Humanism in a Post-humanist Era and its Communist Prospects

In its commitment, Marx's humanism is not philosophical. The anthropocentric human of philosophy or theology is transcendentally impoverished and reduced to a determination in the last instance that is fundamentally material—the human is determined by the real of its "species being." The real is sensuous and physical. Therefore, the opposition of body and mind is inoperative in its classical philosophical sense, as both instances are ultimately determined by the real, insofar as they are material or physical. The human is barely more than an animal, insofar as its determining real is a bundle of muscles and nerves extended in the faculty of "consciousness" that is grounded in the material reality of (human) society. Questions such as "the meaning of life" are meaningless in Marx, as what is required is less suffering and more wellbeing for the human species, for its societies, and for the individuals constituting societies. Similarly, Laruelle reduces the human-in-human to its real, to its mere experience of the lived, while all philosophical constructs of "meaning of human existence" are suspended.

I read Donna Haraway's concept of the "cyborg" as fundamentally the product of a non-philosophical procedure of dualysis brought about by radicalizing the dyad constituted by technology and the organic, rendering its two constituents irreducible to one another. None of the two elements subsumes the other. The human in Donna Haraway's theory of the cyborg is but a product of the interaction between the organic and the technological. Let us radically determine "the technological" as an operation of society, whereas society in the last instance should be determined as the praxis of language. Resorting to psychoanalytic terminology, I would argue that the tendency to expand the possibilities of language—as scientific, and hence technological—is the drive and desire of society in any form. Language is an automaton of self-propagation, and seeks to consolidate and perfect the society. Therefore, the language of science, the purely formal one (including mathematics, computer programming, and other formal languages) and the narrative one (constituting a particular type of ideology or a metaphysical project), unstoppably generates knowledge that results into ever more perfect technological prostheses of the human "species being." Technological progress is propelled by necessity that is constituted by its inherent laws. A socialist or communist framing of technological processes as fundamentally social would consist in aiming at overcoming exploitation and alienation of the physical (Marx) or the organic (Haraway). The technological as speculative or transcendental in the last instance, insofar as it is an operation of language, should foster a sense of physical wellbeing in the human species.

Shulamith Firestone's technological utopism advocates technological development as the means of emancipation of the female body, as determined by nature to such extent that it subjugates the woman as a social being. Her technological agenda seeks to liberate the female human body from its natural vulnerability. In her vision, technology seeks to liberate the female body from pain and politically emancipate her as emancipation of the woman and society as a whole. Firestone's appropriation of Marx, or her posture of thought operating with Marx's textual material, postulates that the determination in the last instance of all exploitation—including class—lies in the sexual exploitation of women.[1] According to Firestone, the exploitation at issue is fundamentally physical as it is related to sexual reproduction and sexuality. Romance is a mere "theology" or ideology that seeks to protect the sexed hierarchy of bodily exploitation, writes Firestone.[2] Firestone says that the exploitation of the body is what determines all forms of exploitation and should be overcome through technology. Donna Haraway argues similarly. If we subscribe to this theory and advocate such a political project, the main question we should address is how can the processes of accelerated technological progress, which in the beginning of the 21st century serves none other than the capital/ists, be overtaken by feminists and the proletariat, by the

---

[1] Shulamith Firestone, *The Dialectic of Sex: The Case for Feminist Revolution* (New York: William Morrow, 1970), 4–5.
[2] Firestone, *The Dialectic of Sex*, 131.

subjugated bodies? The other and perhaps the more fundamental question is "What is the purpose of technological progress today," or differently put, "To whom does it serve nowadays, in the globalized capitalist society of the second decade of the 21st century?"

II. THE CAPITALIST AUTOMATON OF TECHNOLOGICAL AUTOMATION

Nowadays, capital possesses and controls technological progress. Capital dictates its tempo, following the pace of unstoppable acceleration of capital's reproduction (and "growth"). This reality is grounded in the material facts of the ruling economic foundations of technological development, its status of property (owned by the capitalists), and finally in the fact that it is determined by the laws of capitalist social reproduction. Not only are they capitalist, but also they are masculinist, patriarchal, and militarist. The human and its technological prostheses, or the hybrid of technology and the organic that substitutes the human, or in other words Haraway's "cyborg," is the product of the militarist and misogynist capitalism.

> Cyborgs are not reverent; they do not re-member the cosmos. They are wary of holism, but needy for connection-they seem to have a natural feel for united front politics, but without the vanguard party. The main trouble with cyborgs, of course, is that they are the illegitimate offspring of militarism and patriarchal capitalism, not to mention state socialism. But illegitimate offspring are often exceedingly unfaithful to their origins. Their fathers, after all, are inessential.[3]

The question of a socialist revolution in technological development is directly related to the question of the possible turn of the illegitimate children's avowal of their "father's inessentiality," the non-existence of "cosmos," their "wariness of holism" and their "unfaithfulness to their origins." Such a turn would itself be a revolution. A revolutionary movement of this sort would be the grounding gesture what would enable a) an initiation of the political project of expropriation of the processes of technological development as property of a few (the capitalist and the exploiting class), and b) establish social, collective sovereignty in ownership of what is a creation of society and its workers. Technological development would have existed regardless of its finance-based acceleration and commodification for the purposes of "economic

[3] Donna Haraway, "A Cyborg Manifesto," in Donna Haraway, *Simians, Cyborgs, and Women: The Reinvention of Nature* (New York: Routledge, 1991), 151.

growth" in a capitalist society. Technological development is the material product of society as materiality (or physicality) or the "being species." Capitalism reduces it to property as a political concept, which then dictates the economics of alienated labor and of the out of joint, automated, self-regulated, and self-sufficient value (the surplus value or profit).

A socialist turn would consist in a radically materialist reversal of the processes of technological development, by way of grounding it in its fundamental sociality understood as commonality. It would also consist in the dispelling of the specters of surplus value by replacing it (the surplus value) with an always already technologically improved use value for all, distributed according to the immanent laws of the society.

In this way, a society will be able to overcome the inner contradiction of capitalism, consisting in the split between the automated world of speculation, being the spectral universe of pure value (finance), and the material or physical world. The universe of economic or financial value is but the product of a decision made by those in power to arbitrate value and those who are endowed with the sovereignty to institute such decisions. Consequently, in the last instance the automated world of "self-regulated values" is determined by a real that is outside the processes of automation, by a decision that is contingent and physical. Capitalism "behaves" as philosophy because it is the product of "decisionism" that then establishes a self-sufficient universe of speculation pretending to stipulate the real. Technological automation in capitalism mirrors the very logic of capitalism—it is based on the presupposition that it is a self-sufficient universe, and that the physical serves its auto-perfection, rather than the other way around.

> But, once adopted into the production process of capital, the means of labour passes through different metamorphoses, whose culmination is the machine, or rather, an automatic system of machinery (system of machinery: the automatic one is merely its most complete, most adequate form, and alone transforms machinery into a system), set in motion by an automaton, a moving power that moves itself; this automaton consisting of numerous mechanical and intellectual organs, so that the workers themselves are cast merely as its conscious linkages. In the machine, and even more in machinery as an automatic system, the use value, i.e. the material quality of the means of labour, is transformed into an existence adequate to fixed capital and to capital as such; and the form in which it was adopted into the production process of capital, the direct means of labour, is superseded by a form posited by capital itself and corresponding to it. In no way does the machine appear as

the individual worker's means of labour.[4]

The worker, their suffering body and mind, is subjugated not only by a part of humanity, i.e. the capitalist class, but also by the lifeless process of automated value generation. *The automated machine is not a means of production, it is an independent universe parallel to the real of the physical and the lived, whereby no part of the human participates in the former, and is in fact reduced without a remainder to the latter (to a "conscious linkage" in an automated machine).* The idea that the organic (Haraway), the physical (Marx), or the lived (Laruelle) is mere material to the self-sufficient automation is fundamentally capitalistic. The realization of such a political and fundamentally metaphysical project would be the climax and the agony of capitalism itself. It would not liberate women or the proletariat, as these categories will become obsolete. In our post-humanist era, wage laborers will be reduced to wage labor, without a subjectivity to liberate or emancipate itself. In the middle of the second decade of the 21st century, one wonders if in ten or twenty years from now, labor will still be wage labor, or just reduced to labor or organic material used in the universe of cybernetic automation.

One also wonders if there will be—albeit technologically enhanced—bodies to enjoy the fruits of the automated economic production. Would there be only an auto-referential universe of "value production," without a sensuous substratum to absorb the joy and pain issuing from the processes of production? The latter of the two options is the more plausible one unless one admits that the body, the "sensuous and the physical" (Marx), the "organic" (Haraway), or the "lived" (Laruelle) is what ought to be liberated through technological progress.

Marx's text points out consistently that what the body needs to be liberated from is precisely its subjugation by speculation, capitalist automation, and the "universe of values" detached from and exploitative toward the physical. In our era of accelerated capitalism, the socialist goal par excellence is precisely the reversal of the current hierarchy between technology and the organic. Automation is self-sufficient in a fashion that is analogous to the principle of philosophy's sufficiency as diagnosed by Laruelle. Its self-sufficiency implies objectivation of labor (i.e., its abstraction). Both objectivation and abstraction are enabled by the split between speculative reason (of philosophy and capitalism) and "living labor." The function of objectivation, as a fundamentally capitalist operation, is precisely the subjugation of the living labor and its exploitation:

[4] Karl Marx, *Grundrisse: Outlines of the Critique of Political Economy*, trans. Martin Nicolaus (London: Penguin, 1973), 620.

The appropriation of living labour by objectified labour—of the power or activity which creates value by value existing for-itself—which lies in the concept of capital, is posited, in production resting on machinery, as the character of the production process itself, including its material elements and its material motion. The production process has ceased to be a labour process in the sense of a process dominated by labour as its governing unity. Labour appears, rather, merely as a conscious organ, scattered among the individual living workers at numerous points of the mechanical system; subsumed under the total process of the machinery itself, as itself only a link of the system, whose unity exists not in the living workers, but rather in the living (active) machinery, which confronts his individual, insignificant doings as a mighty organism.[5]

The communist or socialist—or the properly Marxian—vision of technological development aims to serve as an emancipating extension of the "living labor" that is made possible by social production. In his impressive rereading of Marx, Michel Henry notes that this concern is the line of consistency and the underlying unifying principle of his entire opus, which is falsely split into "young" and "late Marx." The split between the "late and young Marx," argues Henry, is a falsity and the result of the creation of "Marxism" before the publication of most of Marx's philosophical writings—in particular of *The German Ideology*, which is vindicated in a letter of the "mature Marx" as the work that aimed "to settle accounts with our former philosophical conscience."[6] Emancipation of praxis as subjectivized life is the main political and philosophical concern of Marx, both in his philosophical and economic writings and in his early and late work:

[...] the concepts that remain or that appear in the course of the theoretical elaboration are those that have a fundamental reference to praxis, as, for example, the concepts of the individual, of subjectivity, of life, or reality, and so on.[7]

Shulamith Firestone claims that if the subjugation of living labor is fundamentally physical, then in its last instance it is sexed. Susceptibility to exploitation is related to the body's vulnerability, which is dependent upon the variables of age, health, among others, with gender or sex being the most massive variable among

---

[5] Marx, *Grundrisse: Outlines of the Critique of Political Economy*, 621.
[6] An excerpt from Marx's letter, quoted in Michel Henry, *Marx: A Philosophy of Human Reality* (Bloomington: Indiana University Press, 1983), 10.
[7] Henry, *Marx: A Philosophy of Human Reality*, 12.

them all. However, gendered hierarchy in the exploitation of living labor in the processes of overall social reproduction is not a variable, but rather a constant. This means that the emancipation and liberation of the proletariat is dependent upon the success of a feminist revolution. Technology in service of socialism is at the same time technology in service of feminism.

III. THE STATUS OF HARAWAY'S CYBORG AND FIRESTONE'S TECHNOLOGICAL UTOPIA IN THE SECOND DECADE OF THE 21ST CENTURY

Today, the technological prosthesis of humanity enables the complete remodeling of kinship and the reinvention of gender and sex. The question of the direction in which such processes may go is a matter of political decision. The seemingly autonomous processes of scientific development are in the last instance affected by the real of a political decision. The fact that the political decision is a discursive occurrence does not make its effects less real. The automaton of "machinic reality" is always already affected by the tuche that can result from linguistic activity. However, the linguistic activity at issue is in the last instance determined by the physical, by the real of muscles and nerves that desires, i.e. that needs, enjoys, and/or suffers.

The political is in the last instance physical, and it is that thing against which automation can be defined as its opposite: automation is a reality defined by the absolute absence of political will. The political is automation's exteriority and intervenes into signifying automatism on the principle of *tuché* (chance, coincidence, incidence, incident or the thrust of the real). The political decision reshapes reality by enacting violence that consists in the mere imposition of will, of a particular desire for a change in the processes of signification instituted by virtue of someone's "because I said so." Although the "because I said so" is an enunciation, although it is emptied of transcendental content, it virtually is a bodily extension of the physical instance of wanting, the instance of pure physical desiring that is easily translatable into physical violence if the discursive means do not work.

In our era of neuroscience, it seems naive to insist on the classical philosophical opposition between the physical and the mental. Although neuroscience has not yet offered an explanation of how it is possible that mental processes establish a certain autonomy with respect to the physical, it has nonetheless proven that in the last instance the mental is rooted in the physical. Morality is fundamentally social, and sociality is fundamentally a physical necessity of the human species (and other mammals too), as we can learn from Patricia Churchland's *Braintrust: What Neurosci-*

ence Tells Us About Morality.[8] The political "I want to" and "make it happen because I said so," can dispense of language if one chooses so—they are in the last instance physical because the processes that they generate can suspend all verbal or linguistic justification. Just as morality is a physical necessity linked to the social as yet another product of physical necessity, so too is the political. Politics is nothing else than a more complex organization of a society, according to the ruling morals and power positions for the purposes of regulating its reproduction and homeostasis. In this era of blooming neuroscience, one can safely argue that the continuity between the physical and the mental is scientifically demonstrated. So is the possibility of signifying automation (technology in the digital era) and its independence from the organic. However, does the possibility of automated signification imply superiority of "thought" (the synthetic, non-physical, and "scientifically" created universe) over body? After all, isn't categorization of superior/inferior valuing, and aren't automatons indifferent to values? Therefore, from whose position and from whose point of view is one making the statement about the superiority of the automated systems of computation over the "merely organic" or the "imperfect physical"? From the viewpoint of the machine? Why? Machines are more efficient in production and processes of information than animals (including the human animals), but what are the purposes of that? Is it knowledge as a value per se, as a self-standing meaning, or causa finalis? Perfecting of nature? Either of the two options are in fact what Marx would call a fetish, as either of each is a self-standing, auto-referential, and a self-sufficient abstraction. Unless put in service to the "physical or sensuous" self of the "human species," technology as a purpose in itself is theology.

The machine or automation as an independent, self-enveloped and self-sufficient universe is capitalism out of joint:

> The development of the means of labour into machinery is not an accidental moment of capital, but is rather the historical reshaping of the traditional, inherited means of labour into a form adequate to capital. The accumulation of knowledge and of skill, of the general productive forces of the social brain, is thus absorbed into capital, as opposed to labour, and hence appears as an attribute of capital.[9]

Machinic automation out of joint is endless chatter or endless noise in a schizophrenic split from the material in the last instance,

---

[8] Patricia Churchland, *Braintrust: What Neuroscience Tells Us About Morality* (Princeton: Princeton University Press, 2011).
[9] Marx, *Grundrisse: Outlines of the Critique of Political Economy*, 622.

i.e. the material which is always already there, indifferent to any attempts of the signifying intentionality to reproduce and "perfect" it.

Following Firestone and Haraway's call for feminist and socialist revolution through technology, let us not forget that one should also emancipate the body from the brutal exploitation on the side of (Hegel's) Spirit. Moreover, one should overcome the contradiction immanent to capitalism consisting in what Marx diagnoses as the split between "abstract activity and a belly." The brutal indifference of "abstraction" vis-à-vis the "belly" creates an unsustainable split that will inevitably result in the real of revolt of the suffering bodies. Regardless of the outcomes of such (imagined) revolt, the very logic of capitalism will not only be undermined, but also cancelled; it will consist in what we called in chapter 4 the specific cruelty of capitalism—the full rationalization of any suffering of the body producing "self-exploiting subjects."

Sexuality and reproduction are central coordinates of bodily experiences. That is why I do not see the possibility of feminist emancipation in the capacity of technology to amputate sexuality and reproduction from the female body. A properly Marxian vision of technology's feminist emancipating force would consist in the prosthetic function of liberating the female body from pain, from the physical suffering specific to the female sex, and increasing the potentiality of its active participation in social reproduction (including politics). At this point of technological and cybernetic development, Firestone's warning that technology does not possess immanent emancipatory tendencies, but can rather be used against women and children, has been proven right:

> Though the sex class system may have originated in fundamental biological conditions, this does not guarantee once the biological basis of their oppression has been swept away that women and children will be freed. On the contrary, the new technology, especially fertility control, may be used against them to reinforce the entrenched system of exploitation.[10]

What technology does, and how it does it, affects the entire society and makes it subject to political debate and the field of political struggle. The idea that science and technology possesses some inherent law of functioning and self-regulation resembles the (neo)liberal idea that the capitalist economy is based on laws that constitute a nature in its own right (or as if it emulates nature perfectly). It is for this reason that it should be able to convey its political/ideological/metaphysical presuppositions and its social

---

[10] Firestone, *The Dialectic of Sex*, 10.

consequences in the so-called "commonsensical language." According to Marx, one of the greatest political dangers of the automation of labor is that science would rule the lives and the possibilities of political utterances of the "living labor force":

> The science which compels the inanimate limbs of the machinery, by their construction, to act purposefully, as an automaton, does not exist in the worker's consciousness, but rather acts upon him through the machine as an alien power, as the power of the machine itself.[11]

In other words, science, which "does not exist in the worker's consciousness," operates as an imposition upon and coerces the bodies and minds of wage laborers—it introduces changes in the society of which only those who control the capital can decide in communication with those who speak the esoteric language of their social cast, i.e. the scientists and the academia. A socialist application of technology for the goal of emancipation and liberation of all and everyone in a society presupposes democratic discussion and choices of common interest. Consequently, a socialist practice of technological development is grounded in a political language everyone is "equally intelligent" (Rancière)[12] to take part in (of course, I speak of political grounding, whereas the formal language of science operates according to its own intrinsic rules).

IV. Automation, Capitalist Speculation and (Standard) Philosophy are the Object in the Last Instance of Communist Rebellion, Faithful to Marx's Vision

The three are different instances of the same process that are at the heart of capitalism and determine its inherent laws—the problems of "abstraction." Certainly, Marx is not problematizing a cognitive faculty that is indispensible in the processes of producing knowledge of the surrounding reality. "Abstraction" is a decision about reality that is endowed with a tendency to substitute the "unruly real" (one which "makes no sense" in an accomplished universe of meaning) with a meaning and act as the real that is more perfect than the real itself. In this sense, it operates exactly as philosophy's decisionism, creating an amphibology of the real and "truth" (thought's attempt to possess the real by way of engulfing it). Just as non-standard philosophy operates with the transcendental material of philosophy by succumbing to the dictate of the real, so does Marx invite us to work with ideas that will be in the last in-

---

[11] Marx, *Grundrisse: Outlines of the Critique of Political Economy*, 621.
[12] Jacques Rancière, *The Ignorant Schoolmaster: Five Lessons in Intellectual Emancipation* (Stanford University Press, 1991), 101.

stance determined by the praxis. The real, physical, or sensuous are the determination in the last instance of praxis as opposed to the idealist pretentiousness that rapes the physical (and believes "the physical loves it" and convinces it that it does).

Departing from the sociality that issues directly from the physical, which is first practice and then concept, Marx envisions the socialist system as the most beneficial for all members of a society. What incites productiveness and joy and diminishes pain for each individual in a society is beneficial for the society itself. Marx believes that the prerequisite for such development, and the principle that ensures the desired outcome, is fulfilling the goal that I have determined in the previous chapters as metaphysical (although Marx does not and would not use such determination). Let us remind ourselves, the goal of communism (or its fundament), according to Marx, is "reintegration or return of man to himself, the transcendence of human self-estrangement."[13] In "Communist confession of faith," part of *The Communist Manifesto*, the principle of communism is formulated as follows: "The happiness of the individual is inseparable from the happiness of all, etc." Happiness is a category that is neither abstraction nor materiality. It is radically metaphysical insofar as it belongs to the realm of the necessary mediation of the real, as discussed previously. The goal of communism is to emancipate metaphysics from the rule of philosophy, to radicalize it by rendering it "affected by immanence," by way of producing a posture of thought that would "unilaterally correlate with the real," follow the "syntax of the real" (Laruelle), and be dictated by the "material interests of the human species" (Marx).

The process and also the goal of the communist project is "democracy." *The Communist Manifesto* requires the following "confessions of faith":

Question 16: How do you think the transition from the present situation to community of Property is to be effected?

Answer: The first, fundamental condition for the introduction of community of property is the political liberation of the proletariat through a democratic constitution.

Question 17: What will be your first measure once you have established democracy?

---

[13] Karl Marx, "Third Manuscript: Private Property and Communism," in Karl Marx, *Economic and Philosophical Manuscripts of 1844*, trans. Martin Mulligan (Moscow: Progress Publishers, 1959), available at http://www.marxists.org/archive/marx/works/1844/manuscripts/comm.htm.

Answer: Guaranteeing the subsistence of the proletariat.[14]

The democratization of technological production is a fundamentally social process. If technology is to play a role in the process of the democratization of society, or society's progress toward its general emancipation, democratization of the dialogue on the social and political aspects of technology is necessary. Human emancipation from automation is one of the core concerns of communism and Marxian socialism. Feminist emancipation is its immanent and indispensible aspect.

---

[14] Karl Marx and Frederick Engels, "Manifesto of the Communist Party," in Karl Marx and Frederick Engels, *Selected Works,* Vol. 1 (Moscow: Progress Publishers, 1969), available at https://www.marxists.org/archive/marx/works/1848/communist-manifesto/.

References

A. Printed Secondary Sources

Churchland, Patricia. *Braintrust: What Neuroscience Tells Us about Morality*. Princeton: Princeton University Press, 2011.

Dean, Jodi. *The Communist Horizon*. London: Verso Books, 2012.

Firestone, Shulamith. *The Dialectic of Sex: The Case for Feminist Revolution*. New York: William Morrow and Co., 1970.

Gros, Daniel and Cinzia Alcidi. "The Crisis and the Real Economy." *Intereconomics* 1 (2010): 7–20.

Haraway, Donna. "A Cyborg Manifesto: Science, Technology, and Socialist-Feminism in the Late Twentieth Century." In *Simians, Cyborgs, and Women: The Reinvention of Nature*, 149–181. New York: Routledge, 1991.

Hardt, Michael and Antonio Negri, *Multitudes: War and Democracy in the Age of Empire*. New York: Penguin Putnam, 2004.

Harvey, David. *The Enigma of Capital and the Crisis of Capitalism*. Oxford: Oxford University Press, 2010.

---. *Rebel Cities: From the Right to the City to the Urban Revolution*. London: Verso, 2013.

Henry, Michel. *Marx: A Philosophy of Human Reality*. Bloomington: Indiana University Press, 1983.

Kolozova, Katerina. *The Cut of the Real: Subjectivity in Poststructuralist Philosophy*. New York: Columbia University Press.

Land, Nick. *Fanged Noumena: Collected Writings 1987-2007*. Edited by Ray Brassier and Robin McKay. Faltmouth: Urbanomic, 2011.

Lapavitsas, Costas. *Profiting Without Producing: How Finance Exploits Us All*. London: Verso, 2013.

Laruelle, François. *Philosophie et non-philosophie*. Liège: Pierre Mardaga, 1989.

---. *Théorie des Etrangers: Science des hommes, démocratie et non-psychanalyse*. Paris: Éditions Kimé, 1995.

---. *Introduction au non-marxisme*. Presses Universitaires de France, Paris: 2000.

---. *Ethique de l'Étranger*. Paris: Éditions Kimé, 2000.

---. *Future Christ: A Lesson in Heresy*. Translated by Anthony Paul Smith. London/New York: Continuum, 2010.

---. *From Decision to Heresy: Experiments in Non-Standard Thought*. Translated by Miguel Abreu et al. Falmouth/NewYork: Urbanomic/Sequence, 2012.

---. *Théorie générale des victimes*. Paris: Fayard, 2012.

Laruelle, François, and Anne-Françoise Schmid. "L'identité sexuée." *Identities* 2.3 (2003): 9–61.

Marx, Karl and Friedrich Engels. *The Communist Manifesto*. Translated by Steve Corcoran and Frederick Engels. Progress Publishers: Moscow, 1969.

---. *A Contribution to the Critique of Political Economy*. Translated by S. W. Ryazanskaya. London: Lawrence & Wishart, 1971.

---. *Grundrisse: Outlines of the Critique of Political Economy*. Translated by Martin Nicolaus. New York: Penguin Books, 1973.

Noys, Benjamin. "The War of Time: Occupation, Resistance, Communization." *Identities* X.1-2 (2013): 83–92.

Rancière, Jacques. "Time, Narration and Politics." *Journal for Gender, Politics and Culture: Identities* 11 (2015): 7–18.

---. *The Hatred of Democracy*. Translated by Steve Corcoran. London: Verso, 2006.

---. *The Ignorant Schoolmaster: Five Lessons in Intellectual Emancipation*. Translated by Kristin Ross. Stanford: Stanford University Press, 1991.

Scott, Brett. *The Heretic Guide to Global Finance: Hacking the Future of Money*. London: Pluto Press, 2013.

Smith, Anthony Paul. *A Non-Philosophical Theory of Nature: Ecologies of Thought*. New York: Palgrave Macmillan, 2013.

B. Online Sources

Di Leo, Luca. "Soros Criticizes Obama's Bailouts." *The Wall Street Journal*, March 1, 2010. Available at http://online.wsj.com/news/articles/SB10001424052748704089904575093760994295890.

Financial Crisis Inquiry Commission [FCIC]. The Financial Crisis Inquiry Report: Final Report of the National Commission on the Causes of the Financial and Economic Crisis in the United States. Washington, DC: U.S. Government Publishing Office, 2011. Available at http://www.gpo.gov/fdsys/pkg/GPO-FCIC/content-detail.html.

Marx, Karl. The Theses on Feuerbach. In Karl Marx and Frederick Engels, *The German Ideology*. Translasted by Roy Pascal. London: Lawrence and Wishart, 1938. Available at http://www.marxists.org/archive/marx/works/1845/theses/.

---. *Economic and Philosophical Manuscripts of 1844*. Moscow: Progress Publishers, 1959. Available at https://www.marxists.org/archive/marx/works/download/pdf/Economic-Philosophic-Manuscripts-1844.pdf.

---. *Capital: Volume I*. Translated by Samuel Moore and Edward Aveling, edited by Frederick Engels. Moscow: Progress Publishers, 1887. Available at https://www.marxists.org/

archive/marx/works/1867-c1/.

---. *Capital: Volume II*. Translated by I. Lasker. Moscow: Progress Publishers, 1956. Available at https://www.marxists.org/archive/marx/works/1885-c2/.

---. *Capital Vol. III*. Institute of Marxism and Leninism of USSR: 1959. Available at https://www.marxists.org/archive/marx/works/1894-c3/.

---. "On the Jewish Question." In *Deutsch-Französische Jahrbücher* (February 1844). Available at http://www.marxists.org/archive/marx/works/1844/jewish-question/.

---. *The German Ideology*. Translasted by Roy Pascal. Available at https://www.marxists.org/archive/marx/works/1845/german-ideology/.

Soros, George. "Angela Merkel's Pyrrhic Victory." *Project Syndicate VIII*, October 7, 2013. Available at http://www.project-syndicate.org/commentary/george-soroson-angela-merkel-s-pyrrhic-victory.

Spinoza, Benedict de. *The Ethics*. Translated by R. H. M. Elwes. The Project Gutenberg Etext Publication, 2003. Available at http://www.gutenberg.org/etext/3800.

Srnicek, Nick and Alex Williams. "#Accelerate Manifesto for an Accelerationist Politics." *Critical Legal Thinking* [weblog], May 14, 2012. Available at http://criticallegalthinking.com/2013/05/14/accelerate-ma-nifesto-for-an-accelerationist-politics.

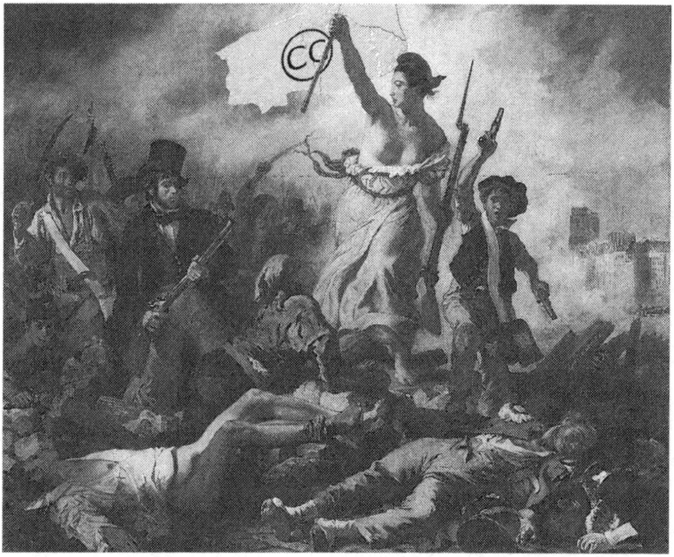
CC

Made in the USA
Middletown, DE
04 February 2016